T0323793

US IMMIGRATION LAWS

UNDER THE

THREAT OF TERRORISM

US IMMIGRATION LAWS

UNDER THE

THREAT OF TERRORISM

Julie Farnam

Algora Publishing
New York

ISBN: 0-87586-373-6 (softcover)
ISBN: 0-87586-374-4 (hardcover)
ISBN: 0-87586-375-2 (ebook)

Library of Congress Cataloging-in-Publication Data —

Farnam, Julie.
    U.S. immigration laws under the threat of terrorism / Julie Farnam.
    p. cm.
    Summary: "An immigration specialist assesses policy changes since the
first World Trade Center bombing in 1993 and the passage of the USA Patriot
Act, and comments on the future of US immigration, including foreign students,
refugees and asylum seekers"
    Includes bibliographical references and index.
    ISBN 0-87586-373-6 (soft cover: alk. paper) — ISBN 0-87586-374-4
(hard cover: alk. paper) — ISBN 0-87586-375-2 (ebook)

    1. Emigration and immigration law—United States. 2. Aliens—United
States. 3. Emigration and immigration—Government policy—United States. 4.
Terrorism—United States—Prevention. I. Title: US immigration laws under
the threat of terrorism. II. Title: United States immigration laws under the
threat of terrorism. III. Title.

    KF4819.F37 2005
    325.73'09'0511—dc22

                    2005000276

Front Cover: Immigration and Border Control in US and Mexico
    US Customs and Border Protection inspectors question a Mexican woman after she used false
documents in order to smuggle two children from Agua Prieta, Mexico into the United States at the
Douglas Arizona Port of Entry. The number of child smuggling cases rose significantly in Arizona and
along the entire border in 2003. Officials repatriated 2,300 Mexican minors in the first nine months of
2003 compared with only 975 in all of 2001.
    © Janet Jarman/Corbis Photographer: Janet Jarman Date Photographed: September 7, 2003
Location Information: Douglas, Arizona, United States

Printed in the United States

To Michael Pepe,
always supportive, loving, and patient

Acknowledgements

A project of this undertaking would not have been possible without the guidance, support, and knowledge of Bennett Savitz of Savitz Law Offices, P.C. in Boston. I am grateful for Bennett's dedication to ensuring that this book provided a well-informed account of the current state of immigration law in the United States. The time spent reviewing and editing on my behalf is greatly appreciated. Without the direction and encouragement provided by Bennett this book would not have become a reality.

I would also like to gratefully acknowledge the contributions of Anh-Hao Phan. Hao was supportive, enthusiastic, and extremely accommodating in obtaining interviews with government personnel. Your generosity was invaluable in the completion of this book and for that I am greatly indebted.

My gratitude also goes to Michael Giacalone for his assistance in aiding my research by providing me with resources valuable in the undertaking of this publication. Michael welcomed me and offered advice that was essential in composing this book.

Larissa, Leanna, and Michael also provided endless hours of critical revisions and manuscript preparation. Thank you for always being willing and available to assist me in my often outlandish undertakings.

Perhaps, most importantly I would like to thank Algora Publishing. I could not find better and more supportive editors. Your commitment to my project is most appreciated. I could not see the realization of my goals without your assistance.

TABLE OF CONTENTS

1. An Era of Terrorism Begins   1

2. Immigration Laws   21

3. The Impact of September 11   53

4. SEVIS and International Students   97

5. Refugees and Asylum Seekers   131

6. The Future of Immigration Policy   159

Index   177

1. An Era of Terrorism Begins

Much attention has been paid to foreign nationals residing in the United States since the terrorist attacks of September 11, 2001, yet in writing a book on the intersection of immigration law and terrorism in the U.S. it is necessary to look back several years, to a time when terrorism on American soil became a reality. With few exceptions, most notably Pearl Harbor in 1941, the United States has largely been exempt from the horrors of terrorism in which other countries experience with more frequency. This fortune changed for the U.S. beginning in 1993 with the World Trade Center bombing. Why the fate of the United States changed is a discussion to be explored at another time. This book instead will examine the United States' response to terrorism through its immigration laws. Foreign nationals committed many of the attacks that occurred against the United States since 1993 and an obvious response to these attacks would be changes in the immigration laws of the country in an effort to counter terrorists from entering the U.S. The challenge that the U.S. faces currently is how to balance the need to keep the country safe from international terrorists and how to welcome those who have legitimate reasons for coming to the country.

Prior to 9/11 there were at least six attacks or planned attacks against the United States, yet only the 1993 WTC bombing was carried out within the borders of the country. Among other attacks that were executed or planned were the bombing of a military site in Saudi Arabia in 1996, the near-simultaneous attacks on U.S. embassies in Kenya and Tanzania in 1998, a planned attack against targets in New York City in 1999, and the 2000 U.S.S. Cole bombing.[1]

The Crowe Commission, which investigated the 1998 embassy bombings in Kenya and Tanzania, reported that between 1987 and 1997 there were more than 225 attacks on U.S. diplomatic installations.[2] The Crowe Commission released its report on the embassy bombings in Kenya and Tanzania in 1999. The 1990s ushered in a new era of terrorism, largely led by al-Qaeda, in which attacks were not state-sponsored, were on a much larger scale, and multiple attacks were often executed simultaneously. Attacks were also occurring on U.S. soil, something that had previously been rare. The 1993 bombing was, at the time, the attack generating the most casualties within the U.S. borders. More than 1,000 people were injured or killed in that attack. The Pearl Harbor attack on December 7, 1941 killed or wounded 1,178 people.[3] These attacks, however, were of a much smaller magnitude than the U.S. Embassy bombing in Kenya in 1998 in which there were over 4,200 casualties. Below is a chart compiled by the Crowe Commission showing the mass casualty numbers from eleven attacks from 1983 to 1998.[4]

---

1. Hill, Eleanor. Testimony before the Hearing on the Intelligence Community's Response to Past Terrorist Attacks Against the United States from February 1993 to September 2001. 8 October 2002.

2. Crowe Commission. "Attacks Against U.S. Diplomatic Installations 1987-1997." U.S. Department of State. January 1999.

3. Department of Defense. 50th Anniversary of World War II Commemorative Committee. *Pearl Harbor: 50th Anniversary Commemorative Chronicle,* "A Grateful Nation Remembers" 1941-1991. Washington: The Committee, 1991.

4. United States. Crowe Commission. "Anti-U.S. Mass Casualty Incidents." Washington, January 1999.

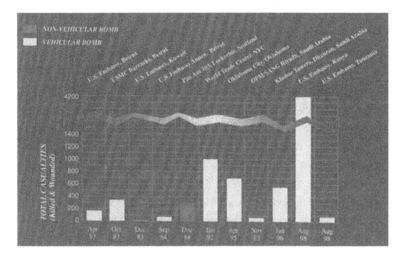

Anti-U.S. Mass Casualty Incidents

Efforts were made by several terrorist organizations to infiltrate the United States during the early 1990s. By setting up organizations within the United States that appeared legitimate, it was easier to bring alien terrorists into the country. One such organization, World and Islamic Studies Enterprise (WISE), was established with the cooperation of the University of Southern Florida (USF).[5] The director of research for WISE, Beshir Musa Nafi, a.k.a. Ahmed Sadiq, was deported from the U.S. in 1996 when it was determined that he was also in a position of authority for the Palestinian Islamic Jihad (PIJ). As discussed at a Senate judiciary hearing, "By utilizing the agreement between USF and WISE as a means of facilitating legitimacy for their activities, the individuals associated with WISE were able to coordinate PIJ activities within the United States free from government scrutiny."[6]

---

5. Emerson, Steven. Testimony before the Senate Committee on the Judiciary. "DOJ Oversight: Preserving Our Freedom While Defending Against Terrorism." Washington, 4 December 2001.

6. *Ibid.*

A similar situation transpired with the United Association for Studies and Research (UASR) based out of Virginia. Musa Abu Marzook, active in UASR, was also a leader within Hamas, a militant Palestinian organization. Abu Marzook came to the U.S. in the 1970s and in 1990 was issued legal permanent residence in the country after winning the diversity lottery. In 1995, while he was trying to reenter the U.S., INS officials arrested Abu Marzook at the request of the Israeli government; Abu Marzook was wanted for his role in murder, attempted murders and conspiracy in connection to the Hamas group.[7]

Hamas, a group that had been designated under the Anti-Terrorism and Effective Death Penalty Act of 1996 as a Foreign Terrorist Organization, has been responsible for attacks throughout the Gaza Strip.[8] Abu Marzook had been head of Hamas's Political Bureau since 1988, yet he received a Green Card in 1990 and was not expelled from the U.S. until 1995, and then only at the request of Israel. This raises questions as to the integrity of the system for determining the eligibility of immigrants that was in use at the time he was allowed to adjust his immigration status. There are possible explanations for allowing Abu Marzook to adjust his status in the U.S., including that his connection to Hamas was unknown by immigration officials or was mistakenly overlooked, or that it was known but, unlikely as is may be, he was not viewed as a threat to the United States.

These earlier incidents with Abu Marzook and Beshir Musa Nafi set the stage for future terrorists to come to the United States, often with grave consequences to this country. In 1990, a man by the name of El Sayyid Nosair assassinated the controversial founder of the Jewish Defense League, Rabbi Meir Kahane. Incidentally, other organizations associated with Kahane, Kahane Chai and Kach, are also listed on the Department of State's list of Foreign Terrorist Organizations, though these organizations became more ordered

7. *Ibid.*

8. Cronin, Ruth Kurth. "Foreign Terrorist Organizations." CRS Report for Congress. 6 February 2004.

and influential under Kahane's son after Meir Kahane's death. (The son was also assassinated, some years after his father.)[9] Officials for Kahane Chai call its inclusion on the list of Foreign Terrorist Organizations "another one-sided, anti-Jewish decree passed by the blatantly anti-Israel State Department," and are actively working to have the group removed from the list.[10]

From one controversial figure and group to another, Nosair's arrest gave the United States a first glimpse into the terrorist network that was working to harm the United States. In fact, some of Nosair's accomplices in his fight for jihad, including Mohammed Salameh and Mahmud Abouhalima, were later connected to the 1993 World Trade Center bombing.[11] Nosair was born in Egypt and married a U.S. citizen; it was not until after his marriage that he became involved in extremist activity, while living in Pittsburgh.[12] This would explain why few flags were raised when Nosair immigrated to the U.S. in the early 1980s.[13]

Nosair, however, was closely connected to Sheik Omar Abdel Rahman, also known as the "Blind Sheik." He was one of the masterminds behind the 1993 WTC bombing as well as the plot to blow up New York City landmarks such as the United Nations headquarters, FBI offices, and other places within the city.[14] He was convicted in 1996, along with El Sayyid Nosair, of seditious conspiracy, a rarely-used law that was enacted in the early 1900s.[15]

---

9. Katzman, Kenneth. "Terrorism: Near Eastern Groups and State Sponsors, 2001." CRS Report for Congress. 10 September 2001.

10. "Kahane.org Responds to the State Department." Kahane.org: The Official Kahane Website. ⟨http://www.kahane.org/response1.html⟩.

11. Miller, John, Michael Stone, and Chris Mitchell. *The Cell.* New York: Hyperion. 2002.

12. McGraw, Seamus. "The Killing of Rabbi Kahane: Jihad in America." Court TV. ⟨http://www.crimelibrary.com/terrorists_spies/terrorists/elsayid_nosair/index.html?sect=22⟩. 2004.

13. Miller, John, Michael Stone, and Chris Mitchell. *The Cell.* New York: Hyperion. 2002.

14. "Sheik Gets Life Sentence in Terror Trial." CNN News. ⟨http://cnn.com/US/9601/terror_trial/update⟩. 17 January 1996.

15. Weiser, Benjamin. "Terror Inquiry Is Using Law on Sedition." *New York Times.* 2 November 2001: B5.

Prior to his involvement with terrorist activities in the U.S., Sheik Rahman was most notably tried and later acquitted of the 1981 assassination of Egyptian president Anwar el-Sadat. He was also arrested in 1989 in Egypt for provoking anti-government riots in the country.[16] The Blind Sheik was issued a tourist visa in Sudan and later was able to adjust his status to that of legal permanent resident in 1991. Sheik Rahman had applied for visas to come to the U.S. a number of times, seven to be exact, and was denied only once. He was, however, questioned on two occasions in regards to his visa applications, once for failing to provide an address where he would be staying while in the U.S. and another time for not having a round-trip ticket to and from the U.S.; but his connections to terrorism never factored into the reviews of his visa applications.[17] The *New York Times* reported that State Department officials claimed "that primitive conditions [in Sudan] may have contributed to his case's being overlooked."[18]

The State Department's Inspector General, Sherman M. Funk, issued a report, of which parts were initially classified, regarding the Department's handling of Sheik Omar Abdel Rahman's visa issuance. The results of this investigation were reported before Congress in a closed hearing in 1993.[19] Sources close to the investigation have affirmed that "the State Department did not notify the INS of the mistake until four months after discovering that it had inappropriately issued the visa to Mr. Abdel Rahman."[20]

Part of the oversight was due to the inadequacy of the visa lookout system employed by the Department of State to check the eligibility or ineligibility of visa applicants to enter the United States.[21] The system, prior to 9/11 generally lacked up-to-date

---

16. "Abdel Rahman, Imprisoned Spiritual Guide to Islamic Extremists." *Agence France Press-English*. 10 April 2002.

17. Jehl, Douglas. "CIA Officers Played Role in Sheik Visas." *New York Times*. 22 July 1993: B1.

18. Jehl, Douglas. "Flaws in Computer Check Helped Sheik Enter U.S." *New York Times*. 3 July 1993: A1.

19. *Ibid.*

20. *Ibid.*

information, as information sharing was often hindered by the lack of communication between government agencies.[22] At the time when the Sheik received his visa, both the State Department and the INS were using a system that relied on data printed on microfiche film, rather than computer files, which makes it more likely that a questionable applicant could be overlooked.[23] In the Sheik's case, it remains a question whether or not his name was even checked in the lookout system when he applied for a tourist visa in 1990.[24]

A push to improve the system occurred shortly after the first WTC bombing in 1993, though serious and effective improvements did not happened until after the attacks of 9/11. A bill introduced in the House by then-Representative Benjamin Gilman (R-NY) stated, "From outdated and inefficient microfiche equipment and lack of basic information sharing, both within the State Department itself, and among U.S. law enforcement agencies and others, the visa lookout system intended to deny potential terrorists, and other criminal elements, easy access to the United States, is badly in need of repair."[25] Sheik Rahman's name was placed in the lookout system in 1987, yet he was issued several U.S. visas.[26]

In a GAO report on the State Department's Information Resource Management it stated in regards to Sheik Rahman obtaining a visa:[27]

---

21. Gilman, Benjamin. "Emergency Plan to Prevent Issuance of Visas to Terrorists." House Concurrent Resolution 119. 13 July 1993.

22.Testimony of Doris Meissner, Former Commissioner, Immigration and Naturalization Service. Before the 9/11 Commission. Seventh Hearing. 26 January 2004.

23.Peterzell, Jay. "How the Sheik Got In." *Time Magazine.* 24 May 1993: 44.

24. Jehl, Douglas. "Flaws in Computer Check Helped Sheik Enter U.S." *New York Times.* 3 July 1993: A1.

25. Gilman, Benjamin. "Emergency Plan to Prevent Issuance of Visas to Terrorists." House Concurrent Resolution 119. 13 July 1993.

26. Jehl, Douglas. "Flaws in Computer Check Helped Sheik Enter U.S." *New York Times.* 3 July 1993: A1.

27. U.S. General Accounting Office. "Department of State IRM: Strategic Approach Needed to Better Support Agency Mission and Business Needs." GAO/AIMD-96-20. Washington: GPO, December 1994.

The Inspector General testified that the first two visas were issued because the Sheik's name was not added to the name-checking system until seven years after it should have been. In 1990, although his name had been added to the system, the Khartoum post issued a visa to the Sheik without checking the microfiche name-check system. According to the Inspector General, because the microfiche system is so time-consuming and cumbersome, there are probably numerous occasions throughout the world where the microfiche is not being checked as required.

It was reported in *Time* Magazine in 1993 that the State Department realized it erred in issuing the visa to Sheik Rahman in 1990. After State was notified by a U.S. official in Egypt, however, that message was never passed on to the INS and with the absence of interconnected databases, the INS was unaware that the visa was revoked and that he was not eligible for entry into the U.S.[28] It remains a question how Sheik Rahman was able to successfully adjust his status and obtain a Green Card a year later. After issuing the Sheik a Green Card in April 1991, the INS later rescinded the card when it learned of his terrorist connections and he was placed in deportation proceedings.[29] When he was issued legal permanent residence in the U.S., one must assume that a similar oversight must have occurred with his application to adjust status as with his application to obtain a visa. He was supposedly placed on a government lookout system several years earlier,[30] yet because of inadequacies in the system he was still able to obtain a visa and later a Green Card.

He was also believed to be connected to the plot to blow up the United Nations Building, the Lincoln and Holland Tunnels, the George Washington Bridge, and the New York headquarters of the FBI.[31] It was this plot for which he was convicted of seditious

28. Peterzell, Jay. "How the Sheik Got In." *Time Magazine.* 24 May 1993: 44.

29. *Ibid.*

30. Jehl, Douglas. "Flaws in Computer Check Helped Sheik Enter U.S." *New York Times.* 3 July 1993: A1.

31. "Punishing Terror, Under Law." *New York Times.* 19 January 1996: A28.

conspiracy, rather than a direct involvement with the 1993 WTC bombing. Though he was accused of involvement in this plot in 1993 and was in deportation proceedings at the time, he was not taken into custody until later that year. The unwillingness for the government to detain him, which Rep. Carolyn B. Maloney suggested was partly due to the medical costs associated with holding the Sheik, as he was in ill health,[32] prompted many, including the Comptroller of New York City Janet Holtzman, to ask Attorney General Janet Reno to arrest him. In a letter to Attorney General Reno she wrote,

> As you may remember, on March 17, I wrote to you to urge the immediate arrest and incarceration of Sheik Rahman pursuant to 8 USC 1252, the law giving the Attorney General the power to arrest and take into custody any alien who is the subject of a deportation proceeding. Sheik Rahman was, at the time, and is now, in deportation proceedings. I renewed the request on March 18 after Immigration and Naturalization Service (INS) Judge Daniel Meissner determined that Sheik Rahman was, in fact, excludable.[33]

The Sheik was put into removal proceedings after his Green Card was revoked. During this time, the Sheik also filed an application for political asylum.[34]

Among the Sheik's followers was a man by the name of Ramzi Yousef. Like his traveling companion, Mohammad Ahmad Ajaj, Yousef entered the U.S. with a fraudulent passport. Immigration officials recognized Yousef's Iraqi passport as a fake and seized it; Yousef responded by immediately filing a claim for asylum from Saddam Hussein's political regime.[35] The immigration official handling Yousef recommended that he be detained while he awaited an asylum hearing, but that request was not heeded because the detention center was filled to capacity. Instead, Yousef was given an

---

32. Maloney, Carolyn B. "Maloney Calls for the Arrest of Sheik Abdel-Rahman." *Congressional Record.* 30 June 1993.

33. Holtzman, Elizabeth. Letter to Attorney General Janet Reno. 25 June 1993.

34. "Why Not Just Deport Him?" *Time Magazine.* 5 July 1993.

35. Miller, Stone, and Mitchell. *The Cell.*

appointment to appear a month later to have his asylum case heard, an appointment to which he never attended.[36]

It may never be known whether the 1993 WTC bombing would have occurred if Yousef had been detained, but it is known that it was a serious error to allow him to freely enter the U.S. This situation also raises larger questions about why the U.S. Immigration Service was unable to detain him. Why was there no space to hold him? This, of course, is a complicated matter that stretches well beyond the immigration officer who handled Yousef's case and the INS in general. At the time that this incident happened, those entering the U.S. to seek asylum were not required to be detained and therefore many were not. This seems acceptable, considering that many who seek asylum do so for valid reasons. However, Yousef proved that some will abuse the system and abuse of the system can harm U.S. citizens; thus, the wisdom of such leniency becomes doubtful.

In addition, the decision not to detain Yousef stems further from the constraints on the immigration system in the U.S., some that come internally and others that are the result of outside forces. Most Americans have little to no connection to the INS and prior to 9/11 failed to recognize the importance of the U.S. Immigration Service. Post 9/11 there is more attention given to immigration and the Immigration Service, but often the focus is on the mistakes the agency made or continues to make, rather than examining the larger reasons behind the agencies' problems. Yousef was not detained because there was no place to detain him, not because the INS did not want to detain him. This failure was a symptom of budgetary constraints placed on the agency, conflicting priorities within the agency as well as outside governmental forces, and ambiguous guidelines.

Yousef was perhaps one of the first terrorists to have an association with Osama Bin Laden, who at the time of the first

---

36. Ekman, Monica M. "Tracing Terror's Roots." *U.S. News and World Report.* 24 February 2003.

WTC bombing was virtually unknown to the majority of the American public. Yousef's uncle, Khalid Shaikh Mohammed, or KSM as he is often known, was one of Osama Bin Ladin's top advisors and he is believed to have been one of the chief masterminds behind the 9/11 attacks. He is al9/11so believed to have provided some of the funding for the 1993 WTC attack.[37] The 9/11 Commission is quoted as saying in regards to Khalid Sheikh Mohammed, "No one exemplifies the model of the terrorist entrepreneur more clearly than Khalid Sheikh Mohammed."[38] It is also interesting to note that like some of the other 1993 WTC terrorists as well as some of the 9/11 hijackers, KSM was at one time a student studying in the U.S., a fact that surely contributed to the tightening of immigration laws as they pertain to international students.[39]

Traveling with Yousef into the U.S. on September 1, 1992 was Mohammad Ahmad Ajaj, who carried luggage containing several manuals on explosives-making and military training.[40] Ajaj had been in the U.S. prior to this trip, and he applied for asylum. Later that same year, Ajaj left the U.S. briefly to visit Pakistan, only to return under a false name with a fraudulent Swiss passport.[41] Even if Ajaj had returned to the U.S. using his genuine name, he still might have encountered problems because he had a case pending with the INS requiring him to be granted permission to leave the U.S., known as advanced parole.[42] Instead, Ajaj traveled on a Pakistan International Airlines flight under the name Mohammed Abid[43] and entered the U.S. with an altered passport with the name Khurram Khan. The passport immediately raised the suspicion of

---

37. 9/11 Commission. *The 9/11 Commission Report.* Washington: GPO, 2004.

38. *Ibid.*

39. *Ibid.*

40. *United States* v. *Ramzi Yousef.* U.S. Court of Appeals 2nd Circuit #98-1355. 4 April 2003.

41. Bernstein, Richard. "Evidence Re-Examined: A Special Report; Questions Raised in One Conviction in Blast at Towers." *New York Times.* 17 October 1994. B1.

42. 8 CFR 223

43. Bernstein, Richard. "Evidence Re-Examined: A Special Report; Questions Raised in One Conviction in Blast at Towers." *New York Times.* 17 October 1994. B1.

the immigration officer at Kennedy International Airport and Ajaj was detained as a result. Ajaj eventually plead guilty to passport fraud and received a six-month sentence, after which he was released. By the time Ajaj left prison, the attack on the WTC had occurred and shortly after his release, he was again detained, this time for his involvement in the bombing.[44]

Also involved in the bombing was Eyad Ismoil, who drove the rental truck that held the bomb that was detonated inside the World Trade Center. Ismoil was a Palestinian man who was born in Kuwait and lived in Jordan.[45] Ismoil originally came to the United States in 1989 to earn his doctorate in engineering at Wichita State University in Kansas.[46] Before enrolling in the program, however, he was required to complete an intensive English-language program at the University.[47] As he originally entered the U.S. on a student visa, his involvement in the WTC bombing helped impel the movement to create a national database that tracks all international students studying in the country. In December 1990, he left the school because he was unable to pay the tuition. From there, he briefly lived in New York City and then began residing in Texas. Upon leaving a university, international students are required to depart from the country. Students who graduate are given a sixty-day grace period to remain in the U.S. or they can apply for a one-year period of work authorization, but because Ismoil left school of his own volition, he was ineligible for these benefits and should have departed shortly after leaving the university.

What Ismoil did instead was to marry an American citizen,[48] which, in turn, made Ismoil immediately eligible to apply for a Green Card. This Green Card, however, would be conditional for

---

44. "The Bombing: Retracing the Steps." *New York Times*. 26 May 1993. B1.

45. McKinley, James C. "Suspect is said to Be Longtime Friend of Bombing Mastermind." *New York Times*. 4 August 1995. B1.

46. "Last World Trade Center Bombing Conspirator Sentenced." CNN News. ‹http:/ /www.cnn.com/US/ 9804/03/wtc.bombing›. 3 April 1998.

47. McKinley, James C. "Suspect is said to Be Longtime Friend of Bombing Mastermind." *New York Times*. 4 August 1995. B1.

48. *Ibid.*

the first two years of the marriage. At the end of the two years, Ismoil and his wife would have to provide the U.S. Immigration Service with evidence that their marriage was a *bona fide* marriage.[49] Evidence could include joint tax filings, joint bank accounts, and birth certificates of children they had together, among other things. Ismoil and his wife, however, divorced before that could be accomplished.

When Ismoil married his American wife, he also became eligible to work legally in the U.S., a benefit that would eventually lead to his undoing. To apply for a work permit and Green Card, Ismoil was required to be fingerprinted by the INS. During a search of a storage facility where the bomb used in the 1993 WTC attack was made, several unidentified fingerprints were found. Also during the investigation it was discovered that Yousef had made several phone calls to Ismoil. Immigration officials were able to unravel the mystery and determine that the unidentified fingerprints were Ismoil's, by comparing them to those on his work authorization card.[50]

While Yousef was the ringleader of the WTC plot and worked closely with Ismoil, El Sayyid Nosair remained a leader, *in absentia*, for the plot, giving advice and guidance to some of the men who were involved in the attack from his jail cell. Two other accomplices in the 1993 bombing were originally recruited and associated with El Sayyid Nosair. In the 1980s, Nosair was active in the al-Kifah Refugee Services Center in Brooklyn. The Center was largely committed to recruiting participants for mujahideen for the Afghan/Soviet war and to fight for jihad in general. Believing that jihad against the U.S. was justified, Nosair recruited others including Mahmud Abouhalima and Mohammed Salameh to join him in his holy war. Along with Nosair, the group of men began paramilitary training where they honed their militant fighting skills as well as

---

49. 8 CFR 216.3

50. McKinley, James C. "Fingerprints Link Suspect to Bombing, Officials Say." *New York Times*. 5 August 1995. A23.

their extreme ideology, traits that would be applied both in the 1990 Kahane murder and the 1993 WTC bombing.[51]

Originally from Egypt, Mahmud Abouhalima obtained a tourist visa to visit Germany in 1981. Seeking to leave Egypt permanently, once he was in Germany Abouhalima sought asylum, a request that was denied in 1982 by German authorities. Not to be deterred, Abouhalima married a German citizen whom he later divorced (in part because she refused to convert to Islam and to have children). Abouhalima divorced his wife in 1985 and shortly thereafter married another German woman. Obtaining tourist visas, the newlyweds headed for the States, never to return to Germany.[52]

Though Abouhalima and his wife entered the United States on tourist visas, they had little intention of returning to their native countries. After their visas expired, Abouhalima fraudulently took advantage of an amnesty provision in the Immigration Reform and Control Act of 1986 (IRCA), which allowed illegal agricultural workers to adjust their status to permanent residents.[53] The law states in part:[54]

SEC. 302. LAWFUL RESIDENCE FOR CERTAIN SPECIAL AGRICULTURAL WORKERS

(a) In general.— (1) Chapter 1 of title II is amended by adding at the end the following new section:

"Special Agricultural Workers"
Sec. 210. (a) Lawful Residence.—

(1) In general.—The Attorney General shall adjust the status of an alien to that of an alien lawfully admitted for

---

51. Miller, Stone, and Mitchell. *The Cell.*

52. Behar, Richard. "The Secret Life of Mahmud the Red." *Time Magazine.* 4 October 1993: 54.

53. Camarota, Steven. Remarks at Cato Institute's Policy Forum. 16 January 2004.

54. P.L. 99-603. Immigration Reform and Control Act. 21 January 1986.

temporary residence if the Attorney General determines that the alien meets the following requirements:

(A) Application period.—The alien must apply for such adjustment during the 18-month period beginning on the first day of the seventh month that begins after the date of enactment of this section.

(B) Performance of seasonal agricultural services and residence in the United States.—The alien must establish that he has—

(i) resided in the United States, and

(ii) performed seasonal agricultural services in the United States for at least 90 man-days, during the 12-month period ending on May 1, 1986. For purposes of the previous sentence, performance of seasonal agricultural services in the United States for more than one employer on any one day shall be counted as performance of services for only 1 man-day.

(C) Admissible as immigrant.—The alien must establish that he is admissible to the United States as an immigrant, except as otherwise provided under subsection (c)(2).

(2) Adjustment to permanent residence.—The Attorney General shall adjust the status of any alien provided lawful temporary resident status under paragraph (1) to that of an alien lawfully admitted for permanent residence on the following date:

(A) Group 1.—Subject to the numerical limitation established under subparagraph (C), in the case of an alien who has established, at the time of application for temporary residence under paragraph (1), that the alien performed seasonal agricultural services in the United States for at least 90 man-days during each of the 12-month periods ending on May 1, 1984, 1985, and 1986, the adjustment shall occur on the first day after the end of the one-year period that begins on the later of (I) the date the alien was granted such temporary resident status, or (II) the day after the last day of the application period described in paragraph (1)(A).

(B) Group 2.—In the case of aliens to which subparagraph (A) does not apply, the adjustment shall occur on the day after the last day of the two-year period that begins on the later of (I) the date the alien was granted such temporary resident status, or (II) the day after the last day of the application period described in paragraph (1)(A).

(C) Numerical limitation.—Subparagraph (A) shall not apply to more than 350,000 aliens. If more than 350,000 aliens meet the requirements of such subparagraph, such subparagraph shall apply to the 350,000 aliens whose applications for adjustment were first filed under paragraph (1) and subparagraph (B) shall apply to the remaining aliens.

(3) Termination of temporary residence.—During the period of temporary resident status granted an alien under paragraph (1), the Attorney General may terminate such status only upon a determination under this Act that the alien is deportable.

The problem with Abouhalima's request for permanent residence based on Section 302 of IRCA was that he was a cab driver in New York City and at no point in his stay in the United States had he been employed in the agricultural field.[55]

His misuse of this provision might have gone unnoticed if not for his involvement in the WTC bombing. Abouhalima aided the WTC bombing by purchasing some of the ingredients used to make the bomb that was used on February 26, 1993.[56] Since this abuse of §302 by Abouhalima, there has been much outcry regarding immigration provisions that give amnesty to some illegal immigrants.

Abouhalima's case has been the topic of much discussion since late 2004 because of President George W. Bush's similar proposal allowing illegal immigrants to apply for legal status. The problem

---

55. Camarota, Steven. Remarks at Cato Institute's Policy Forum. 16 January 2004.

56. Testimony of J. Gilmore Childers and Henry J. DePippo before the Senate Judiciary Committee Subcommittee on Technology, Terrorism, and Government Information. 24 February 1998.

lies not with the provision itself or provisions similar in scope to IRCA's §302, but in properly applying its benefits. Section §302(b)(3) outlines elements necessary to prove eligibility, documents that Abouhalima either did not have or obtained fraudulently. The question of whether and how these documents were reviewed as part of his application for permanent residency is a key component in determining why he was granted permanent residency when he had no claim to agricultural work in the United States.

There have been several forgiving provisions introduced into immigration law, most notably Section 245(i) of the Immigration and Nationality Act. In its most recent incarnation, 245(i) allowed those who had entered the U.S. illegally or who did not maintain their status to adjust their status to that of permanent resident if a petition was filed on their behalf between January 14, 1998 and April 30, 2001; if they could prove they were physically present in the U.S. on December 21, 2000; and if they agree to pay a $1000 penalty fee.[57]

So-called amnesty provisions, as they are commonly termed, raise a larger question as to why those who are not in the U.S. legally or who are otherwise ineligible to become permanent residents should be allowed to adjust their status. What message does this send to immigrants who play by the rules and go through all the (often complicated) processes to come to the U.S. and stay in the country legally? Abouhalima's case fueled this debate, one that will surely continue as the President introduces additional measures to grant unauthorized immigrants opportunities to extend their stay in the U.S.

Before being granted permanent residency, Abouhalima was in the U.S. illegally as he had overstayed his tourist visa. Similarly, Mohammed Salameh was also in the U.S. illegally after overstaying his tourist visa by more than four years at the time of the 1993 WTC bombing.[58] A native of Jordan, Salameh rented the Ryder truck used

---

57. 8 CFR 245(i).
58. "Another Hazard of Illegal Immigration." *Human Events.* 4 November 2002.

in the bombing. He is perhaps one of the most inept of terrorists, as he returned to the rental store after the bombing to ask for his deposit back. His involvement in the bombing fueled the debate about illegal immigration.

Post 9/11, illegal immigrants have come to be seen as synonymous with terrorists, although that is not the case. There are thousands of illegal immigrants within the United States, a situation that existed well before Salameh entered the country, before the 1993 WTC bombing, and before 9/11. The media and anti-immigration organizations are quick to conclude that illegal immigrants are threatening the American people. In an article that appeared in *Human Events*, the author worried about "risks Americans must run because the federal government does not enforce its immigration laws: an increased threat of violent crime, including terrorism."

It is both irresponsible and unjustified to draw the conclusion that illegal immigration increases the threat of violent crime. While illegal immigration is excessive in some parts of the country and immigration laws should be more thoroughly enforced, increased violence and terrorism are not direct or even indirect results of illegal immigration. It is important not to forget that Americans engage in violent crime and some American citizens, such as Timothy McVeigh and Terry Nichols, are terrorists also.

A fellow U.S. citizen (though naturalized, unlike Timothy McVeigh and Terry Nichols who were citizens at birth), Nidal Ayyad worked with Abouhalima, Yousef, Ismoil, and Salameh to try to destroy the WTC. Unlike many of his co-conspirators, Nidal Ayyad appeared to be stable and productive in American society. Ayyad was, prior to his involvement with the 1993 WTC bombing, the epitome of the American Dream. Having arrived in the U.S. from Kuwait in 1985, Ayyad worked hard to earn his chemical engineering degree from Rutgers University,[59] gaining knowledge

---

59. John V. Parachini. *Toxic Terror: Assessing Terrorist Use of Chemical and Biological Weapons.* Ed. Jonathan B. Tucker. Cambridge, MA: MIT Press. 2000.

that would be key in mixing the ingredients used in the bomb at the WTC. Upon graduation in 1991, Ayyad secured a position at AlliedSignal,[60] an engineering company that merged with Honeywell in the 1990s. Ayyad became a naturalized citizen in 1991.[61]

Ayyad and his accomplices in many ways introduced the United States to terrorism. By exploiting flaws within the system, particularly those within immigration, dangerous individuals were able to enter the United States and work to destroy the country through terrorist acts. Lessons that should have been learned in 1993, particularly in the case of Sheik Omar Abdel Rahman who was on a terrorist watchlist yet was given a U.S. visa and was then granted permanent residency, would come back to haunt the U.S. on 9/11, with most of the hijackers having violated their immigration statuses.

Balancing the security needs of the U.S. with the efforts to welcome immigrants must be a coordinated effort. The weight of this charge does not rest solely of the shoulders on the immigration services of the country, it requires input and cooperation from several agencies and departments within the government as well as the support of Congress and the American people. The United States is a country of immigrants and now more than ever it is important to embrace the knowledge and perspectives that can be gained from welcoming immigrants into our country.

---

60. "Excerpts From Complaint Against Nidal Ayyad." *New York Times*. 11 March 1993. B1.
61. Smolowe, Jill. "The $400 Bomb." *Time Magazine*. 22 March 1993: 40.

2. IMMIGRATION LAWS

The basis for U.S. immigration law is the Immigration and Nationality Act (INA). Created in 1952, it drastically changed U.S. immigration policy and remains the foundation of immigration law in this country, though the Act has been amended on several occasions. To fully understand how the immigration laws in the U.S. have changed under the threat of terrorism, it is important to understand what is being altered. All of the Acts discussed have amended the INA in some way; therefore, no discussion on immigration law changes would be complete without a brief introduction of the Act that still today provides the heart of U.S. immigration policy.

Introduced to Congress by Senator Patrick A. McCarran, the bill consolidated many of the immigration laws that existed at the time.[1] Unlike previous immigration laws, however, the INA allowed all nationalities to be eligible for naturalization. Prior to the INA laws were implemented such as the Chinese Exclusion Act of 1882[2] and the Immigration Act of 1926 aimed at excluding the Japanese,[3]

---

1.   Aleinikoff, Thomas Alexander, David A. Martin, and Hiroshi Motomura. *Immigration and Citizenship: Process and Policy*. St. Paul, MN: West Publishing Co. 2003.

that barred immigrants of certain nationalities from becoming American citizens. The INA was the first immigration law that eliminated race as a factor in determining eligibility for citizenship. Similarly, under the INA gender was no longer a factor in determining qualification for citizenship.[4]

With the INA, classification of nonimmigrants were increased while also raising the number of those eligible to immigrate permanently to the U.S. by creating the family preference system, revising the quota system, and giving preference to skilled immigrants whose services were needed in the U.S.[5]

The INA was also one of the first laws to expand the application of exclusion and deportation, something that would be overhauled under the Illegal Immigration Reform and Immigrant Responsibility Act of 1996. Additionally, the INA was one of the first laws that created a national system for immigrants to be used by "enforcement and security agencies."[6]

Among laws that would amend the INA in light of terrorist threats would be the Antiterrorism and Effective Death Penalty Act of 1996 (AEDPA). Title three of AEDPA discussed the First Amendment right of freedom of assembly. This is particularly important because since 9/11 close attention has been paid to international organizations, their potential links to terrorism and their fundraising techniques. The USA PATRIOT Act in 2001 would later revisit this concept.

AEDPA was the result of two terrorist attacks on America's soil, the 1995 Oklahoma City Bombing, committed by American

2. Chinese Exclusion Act of May 6, 1882 (22 Statutes-at-Large 58). U.S. Citizenship and Immigration Services. ‹http://uscis.gov/graphics/shared/aboutus/statistics/legishist/450.htm›. 9 June 2003.

3. Immigration Act of May 26, 1924 (43 Statutes-at-Large 153). U.S. Citizenship and Immigration Services. ‹http://uscis.gov/graphics/shared/aboutus/statistics/legishist/470.htm›. 9 June 2003.

4. Immigration and Nationality Act of June 27, 1952 (INA) (66 Statutes-at-Large 163). U.S. Citizenship and Immigration Services. ‹http://uscis.gov/graphics/shared/aboutus/ statistics/LegisHist/511.htm›. 9 June 2003.

5. *Ibid.*

6. *Ibid.*

citizens, and the 1993 WTC bombing, committed by foreign nationals. Since 9/11, however, this act has taken on new meaning, much of which is being applied to combating foreign terrorists in the United States. Section 302 of the AEDPA amends §219 of the INA by outlining how foreign organizations are to be designated as terrorist organizations. It states:

SEC. 302. DESIGNATION OF FOREIGN TERRORIST ORGANIZATIONS.

(a) In general — Chapter 2 of title II of the Immigration and Nationality Act (8 U.S.C. 1181 et seq.) is amended by adding at the end the following:

SEC. 219. DESIGNATION OF FOREIGN TERRORIST ORGANIZATIONS.

(a) Designation

(1) In general — The Secretary is authorized to designate an organization as a foreign terrorist organization in accordance with this subsection if the Secretary finds that —

(A) the organization is a foreign organization;

(B) the organization engages in terrorist activity (as defined in section 212(a)(3)(B)); and

(C) the terrorist activity of the organization threatens the security of United States nationals or the national security of the United States.

(2) Procedure

(A) Notice — Seven days before making a designation under this subsection, the Secretary shall, by classified communication —

(i) notify the Speaker and Minority Leader of the House of Representatives, the President pro tempore, Majority Leader, and Minority Leader of the Senate, and the members of the relevant committees, in writing, of the intent to designate a foreign organization under this subsection, together with the findings made under paragraph (1) with respect to that organization, and the factual basis therefore; and

(ii) seven days after such notification, publish the designation in the Federal Register.

(B) Effect of Designation

(i) For purposes of section 2339B of title 18, United States Code, a designation under this subsection shall take effect upon publication under subparagraph (A).

(ii) Any designation under this subsection shall cease to have effect upon an Act of Congress disapproving such designation.

(C) Freezing of Assets — Upon notification under paragraph (2), the Secretary of the Treasury may require United States financial institutions possessing or controlling any assets of any foreign organization included in the notification to block all financial transactions involving those assets until further directive from either the Secretary of the Treasury, Act of Congress, or order of court.

(3) Record

(A) In general — In making a designation under this subsection, the Secretary shall create an administrative record.

(B) Classified Information — The Secretary may consider classified information in making a designation under this subsection. Classified information shall not be subject to disclosure for such time as it remains classified, except that such information may be disclosed to a court ex parte and in camera for purposes of judicial review under subsection (c).

(4) Period of Designation

(A) In general — Subject to paragraphs (5) and (6), a designation under this subsection shall be effective for all purposes for a period of 2 years beginning on the effective date of the designation under paragraph (2)(B).

(B) Redesignation — The Secretary may redesignate a foreign organization as a foreign terrorist organization for an additional 2-year period at the end of the 2-year period referred to in subparagraph (A) (but not sooner than 60 days prior to the termination of such period) upon a finding that the relevant circumstances described in paragraph (1) still exist. The procedural requirements of paragraphs (2) and (3) shall apply to a redesignation under this subparagraph.

(5) Revocation by Act of Congress — The Congress, by an Act of Congress, may block or revoke a designation made under paragraph (1).

(6) Revocation based on Change in Circumstances

(A) In general — The Secretary may revoke a designation made under paragraph (1) if the Secretary finds that —

(i) the circumstances that were the basis for the designation have changed in such a manner as to warrant revocation of the designation; or

(ii) the national security of the United States warrants a revocation of the designation.

(B) Procedure — The procedural requirements of paragraphs (2) through (4) shall apply to a revocation under this paragraph.

(7) Effect of Revocation — The revocation of a designation under paragraph (5) or (6) shall not affect any action or proceeding based on conduct committed prior to the effective date of such revocation.

(8) Use of Designation in Trial or Hearing — If a designation under this subsection has become effective under paragraph (1)(B), a defendant in a criminal action shall not be permitted to raise any question concerning the validity of the issuance of such designation as a defense or an objection at any trial or hearing.

(b) Judicial Review of Designation

(1) In general — Not later than 30 days after publication of the designation in the Federal Register, an organization designated as a foreign terrorist organization may seek judicial review of the designation in the United

States Court of Appeals for the District of Columbia Circuit.

(2) Basis of Review — Review under this subsection shall be based solely upon the administrative record, except that the Government may submit, for ex parte and in camera review, classified information used in making the designation.

(3) Scope of Review — The Court shall hold unlawful and set aside a designation the court finds to be —

(A) arbitrary, capricious, an abuse of discretion, or otherwise not in accordance with law;

(B) contrary to constitutional right, power, privilege, or immunity; or

(C) in excess of statutory jurisdiction, authority, or limitation, or short of statutory right.

(4) Judicial Review Invoked — The pendency of an action for judicial review of a designation shall not affect the application of this section, unless the court issues a final order setting aside the designation.

This section of the AEPDA laid the foundation for future legislation that would be enacted and expanded to include domestic organizations as well after 9/11. Designation as a terrorist organization can result in inadmissibility of foreign nationals associated with those organizations. Prior to 9/11, the President used this section to declare Hezbollah and the Popular Front for the Liberation of Palestine (PFLP) terrorist organizations.[7]

While the President has used this section to make designations of foreign terrorist groups, this responsibility is usually executed by the Secretary of State. Designations are for two-year periods, with the possibility of a two-year extension or the possibility of a withdrawal of designation. It is noteworthy that, although

---

7. Doyle, Charles. "Antiterrorism and Effective Death Penalty Act of 1996: A Summary." Federation of American Scientists. ‹http://www.fas.org/irp/crs/96-499.htm›. 3 June 1996.

designations are made in two-year increments, members of these organizations only have thirty days from the date of designation to appeal.

Under $302 of the AEPDA, the Secretary of State created the Terrorism Exclusion List. Based on the list of Foreign Terrorist Organizations (FTO),[8] the original Terrorism Exclusion List of 1997 included thirty foreign organizations.[9] The Terrorism Exclusion List was updated on April 29, 2004 to include nearly sixty organizations from all over the world, including organizations based in the United States such as the Anarchist Faction for Overthrow. Although the AEPDA outlines how terrorist organizations are designated by the Secretary of State, it does not specify the criteria that are used to determine what groups should be included on the Terrorism Exclusion List.

This information would possibly shed light on why groups such as the Ku Klux Klan and the Army of God, both with histories of terrorizing and murdering American citizens, are not on the Terrorist Exclusion List. Many organizations were added after 9/11, yet only one is domestic. Has September 11th distorted the U.S perception of organizations that have the potential to harm its citizens, creating the assumption that the most dangerous terrorists are foreigners?

Perhaps what is most worrisome about this section of the AEDPA from an immigration and legal standpoint is that $302(a)(8) makes it impossible for an alien who has been found inadmissible or removable from the U.S. because of an affiliation to a group listed on the Terrorist Exclusion List to object to the ruling on the basis that he (or she) was unjustly or incorrectly accused of association. This provision has grave implications for American citizens as well, though most post-9/11 focus has been on noncitizens. This provision

---

8. "CDI Fact Sheet: Current List of Designated Foreign Terrorist Organizations." Center for Defense Information. ‹http://www.cdi.org/terrorism/terrorist.cfm#l›. 27 March 2003.

9. Office of the Coordinator for Counterterrorism. "Fact Sheet: Designation of Foreign Terrorist Organizations." U.S. Department of State. 8 October 1997.

is not limited to use on noncitizens and while few flags are raised when this provision of AEDPA is utilized with foreign nationals, the provision virtually strips Americans of due process rights.

Furthermore, the lack of clarity in how a group comes to be designated a terrorist organization leaves it wide open for abuse. As discussed in an article that appeared in *The Nation*, "The sweeping powers granted the State Department give the federal government the ability to ban and effectively close down any cantankerous group that it doesn't like."[10] Without specific guidelines outlined in the law, as the article also points out, the process of designating groups can become highly politicized, shaped by lobbyists and the relationship the U.S. has with foreign governments.[11] Furthermore, classified information may be used in determining who will be listed. While this in itself is not problematic, it becomes so when that group seeks judicial review in which that classified information can be used without their knowing what it contains.

This was the case with foreign national Nasser Ahmed, a translator for Sheik Omar Abdel Rahman who was convicted of plotting terrorist acts in New York City, when he was accused of terrorist ties himself. Though Ahmed was exonerated of any terrorist ties, it proved difficult to defend against the accusations because they were classified. As CNN News reported, "Civil liberties and Arab-American groups have accused the INS of denying due process to about two dozen suspects of Arab descent by jailing them without allowing them to confront the evidence against them."[12]

The use of secret evidence in terrorism-related cases has been debated in recent years because many argue that it violates due process rights. In 1999 a Federal District judge ruled that the due process rights of Hany Mahmoud Kiareldeen, a Palestinian who originally entered the U.S. as a student, but then applied for an

---

10. Dreyfuss, Robert. "Colin Powell's List." *The Nation.* 274, 11. 25 March 2002.
11. *Ibid.*
12. "Released Immigrant Speaks Out Against Use of Secret Evidence." CNN News. ‹http://www.cnn.com/US/9911/30/secret.evidence/index.html›. 30 November 1999.

adjustment of status after marrying an American citizen, were violated because of the use of secret evidence. Beth Lyon in an article written for Findlaw.com made this point most poignantly when she wrote:[13]

> To enter a strange chapter in America's history, imagine that you are a lawyer sitting in a courtroom next to your client, an indigent refugee seeking political asylum from his country's dictatorial regime. Your opponent calls the government's first witness, a police officer who is going to explain why the government believes your client is a terrorist. The government attorney, the police officer, and the judge all get up and walk into another room, leaving your client (and you) to guess what the judge is hearing and seeing. Subsequently, the judge announces that, based on the secret testimony and classified documents, your client will have to remain in jail indefinitely. In addition, large portions of the judge's written opinion explaining the decision are redacted because they contain classified information.

Judge William H. Walls, who issued the opinion of the court, stated, "The government's reliance on secret evidence violates the due process protections that the Constitution directs must be extended to all persons within the United States, citizens and resident aliens alike."[14] In a surprising move, the Department of Justice released a statement shortly after the ruling stating that it did not intend to appeal the court's finding. It said, "the Board [of Immigration Appeals] agreed that the government's evidence, which was classified, by itself may have justified a belief that Kiareldeen posed a threat to the national security. But, the Board found that Kiareldeen offered evidence sufficient to overcome that concern."[15]

There are several provisions within AEDPA that apply specifically to aliens. Among them, §432 requires the INS to create a "criminal alien identification system."[16] Inclusion of this section is

---

13. Lyon, Beth. *Secret Evidence.* FindLaw's Writ. ‹http://writ.news.findlaw.com/ scripts/ printer_friendly.pl?page=/commentary/20000621_lyon.html›. 21 June 2000.

14. *Kiareldeen v. Reno,* 71 F.Supp. 2d 402 (D.N.J.1999)

15. "Statement by the Justice Department on the Case Against Hany Kiareldeen." U.S. Department of Justice. Washington, 26 October 1999.

16. S.735. Antiterrorism and Effective Death Penalty Act of 1996. §432.

most probably related to the fact that one of the masterminds of the 1993 WTC bombing was Sheik Omar Abdel Rahman, also known as "the Blind Sheik." Sheik Omar, a friend of Osama bin Laden, obtained a Sudanese passport and a U.S. tourist visa in 1991, although he was on a terrorist watch list. In addition to obtaining a visa, he was able to enter the United States, where he proceeded to recruit followers to his jihad movement.[17] Clearly, safeguards available to prevent terrorists from entering the U.S. were not utilized by either the Consular Officers under the Department of State responsible for the issuance of visas or the immigration officials under the INS, who are responsible for reviewing eligibility for admission into the country.

This, in turn, raises several points. Though it is important to have a resource available to immigration, consular, and law enforcement officials regarding the criminality of foreign nationals, such a resource, as the Blind Sheik's case illustrates, is only as good as those who use it. If a system such as the one proposed in §432 of AEDPA is not used or updated regularly, the system will be mostly useless and will do little to prevent terrorism. Moreover, there is a distinction (which after 9/11 is often misinterpreted) between a criminal and a terrorist. Not all criminals are terrorists, and while criminal aliens are not contributing to the betterment of the U.S., that does not imply that they are trying to destroy the country through terrorist means.

The year 1996 ushered in a series of laws to reform immigration in the United States. In addition to AEDPA was the Illegal Immigration Reform and Immigrant Responsibility Act (IIRIRA), which made sweeping changes to immigration policies within the country. IIRIRA drastically changed the landscape of immigration law by implementing changes in border control, document fraud dealings, admissibility procedures, removal processes, asylum and refugee law, with implications for international students, and visas

---

17. "Abdel Rahman, Imprisoned Spiritual Guide to Islamic Extremists." Agence France Presse-English. 10 April 2002.

and consular procedures in general. This law is perhaps the biggest overhaul of the U.S.'s immigration system since the INA and it was done in large part because of the 1993 WTC bombing, as well as the discovery that other foreign nationals were planning to execute a series of terrorist attacks within the United States.[18]

Much of the earlier sections of IIRIRA focus on the need for increased border security, something that remains a challenge several years after IIRIRA and 9/11. Section 101 of the Act increases the number of border agents by at least one thousand full time personnel, which are to be dispersed along the U.S. borders in numbers proportional to the number of illegal immigrants crossing the border at those locations. Along with increasing the number of immigration officials patrolling the border of the country, IIRIRA proposes to increase the barriers between California and Mexico in an effort to keep out illegal immigrants. This, combined with the authorization for additional access to technological resources such as night-vision goggles, was intended to decrease the number of illegal immigrants crossing into the United States. As explored more fully in chapter six, illegal immigration has not been deterred by IIRIRA.

Under IIRIRA, certain provisions require that non-governmental entities be responsible for the enforcement of immigration laws. This is apparent with the Student and Exchange Visitor Information System (SEVIS), the national database tracking international students and exchange visitors as mandated under §641 of the Act. As school officials have been required to maintain the SEVIS database, airlines have also been required by the U.S. government to take on a more active role in enforcing immigration laws by prescreening passengers to ensure that they have proper documentation to enter the United States.

Even before 9/11, there had been much focus on the airline industry and how to better secure the United States from those

---

18. "Sheik Gets Life Sentence in Terror Trial." CNN News. ‹http://www.cnn.com/US/9601/terror_trial/update›. 17 January 1996.

arriving by air. Section 123 of IIRIRA required that the Attorney General identify the five foreign airports from which visitors most often enter the United States and set up prescreening inspection stations by November 2000. Fifteen airports currently participate in the prescreening process, and most of them began participating after 9/11.[19]

Airlines had long been a focus of terrorism. In a 2000 House Subcommittee meeting, Admiral Cathal Flynn, Associate Administrator for Civil Aviation Security, stated, "The relationship between Osama bin Laden, who was behind these terrorist attacks [in Kenya and Tanzania], and Ramzi Yousef, who was convicted of bombing the World Trade Center in New York and attempting to place bombs on a dozen U.S. air carrier flights in the Asia-Pacific region in 1995, exemplifies the continuing tangible threat to civil aviation."[20]

Among systems created to enhance aviation security was the program known as the Computer-Assisted Passenger Prescreening System (CAPPS). With CAPPS, the baggage of some passengers who meet criteria developed by counterterrorism officials is subject to additional screening.[21] This program gained notoriety after 9/11 when it was learned that Mohamed Atta, the ringleader of the 9/11 attacks, was selected for CAPPS review.[22] But Jane Garvey, speaking before the 9/11 Commission, showed that the system was flawed. "On Sept. 10, CAPPS was used only to focus efforts to counter explosive sabotage."[23] She also noted that the majority of the 9/11 hijackers did not carry any luggage and without luggage there was little the system could do to check whether they were a threat. [24]

---

19. Wasem, Ruth Ellen, et. al. "Border Security: Inspection Practices, Policies, and Issues." CRS Report for Congress. 26 May 2004.

20. Flynn, Cathal. Testimony Before the U.S. House Subcommittee Meeting on Aviation on Aviation Security. 16 March 2000.

21. Ibid.

22. 9/11 Commission. 9/11 Commission Report. Washington: GPO, 2004.

23. Garvey, Jane. Testimony Before the 9/11 Commission. 22 May 2003.

24. Loy, James M. Testimony Before the 9/11 Commission. 27 January 2004.

Under IIRIRA, airlines are also required to prescreen immigration documents to aid in the detection of fraud. Funding for the training of airline personnel to detect fraud is allocated under the Act; failure to comply with the regulations outlined in IIRIRA can result in the airline's being forbidden from operating in the United States. As the Department of Justice stated, "In this respect, the international airline industry serves as an important part of the Government's control strategy in preventing an improperly documented passenger from flying to the United States."[25] With IIRIRA and other acts instituted after 9/11, non-governmental entities, i.e. the airlines and schools, were required to take on responsibilities to enforce immigration laws, a responsibility that was previously reserved for the government.

Preventing immigrants from entering the U.S. by fraudulent means is a central focus of much of IIRIRA. In addition to added requirements for airlines to screen passengers to ensure they are not trying to enter the U.S. illegally, several sections of IIRIRA are dedicated to the prevention of alien smuggling. It is important to distinguish between alien smuggling and human trafficking. Unlike alien smuggling, human trafficking often involves coercion and those being trafficked may have been taken against their will or may be forced to engage in activities without their consent. Alien smuggling, on the other hand, is a profitable enterprise in which aliens willfully pay to be smuggled into the country.[26]

Now that terrorism is considered a significant threat to the United States, attention must be paid to the network of alien smugglers that work to bring foreign nationals, some of whom may be dangerous, into the country. As Charles DeMore, Interim Direct of Investigations for ICE, said at a Senate Judiciary hearing in 2003, "This emphasis recognizes that terrorists and their associates are likely to align themselves with specific alien smuggling networks to

---

25. "INS and Airline Industry Relations." Report Number I-2000-020. U.S. Department of Justice. Washington: GPO, September 2000.

26. DeMore, Charles. Testimony Before the Senate Judiciary Committee. 25 July 2003.

obtain undetected entry into the United States."[27] Furthermore, an article written for *Time Magazine* regarding illegal immigrants in the U.S., pointed out that Fort Huachuca, Arizona home to the U.S. Army's Intelligence Center, which trains military officials, is "a thoroughfare for illegal aliens and drug smugglers, with mountains on the base providing a safe haven."[28] Even before 9/11, IIRIRA recognized this threat and put focus on prevention and prosecution of alien smugglers. Provisions under IIRIRA that address this issue include authorizing wire taps of suspected alien smugglers, increasing the penalties for those convicted in smuggling, expanding covert surveillance, and increasing the racketeering offenses related to alien smuggling.[29]

Often, with alien smuggling, a fee is paid to obtain illegal documentation, such as work permits, as well as to cover the actual covert travel. Sections 211 and 212 of IIRIRA substantially increase the penalties for using fraudulent government-issued documents and expands the definition of document fraud to include:[30]

> (5) to prepare, file, or assist another in preparing or filing, any application for benefits under this Act, or any document required under this Act, or any document submitted in connection with such application or document, with knowledge or in reckless disregard of the fact that such application or document was falsely made or, in whole or in part, does not relate to the person on whose behalf it was or is being submitted, or

> (6)(A) to present before boarding a common carrier for the purpose of coming to the United States a document which relates to the alien's eligibility to enter the United States, and (B) to fail to present such document to an immigration officer upon arrival at the United States port of entry.

---

27. *Ibid.*

28. Barlett, Donald L. and James B. Steele. "Who Left the Door Open?" *Time Magazine.* 20 September 2004: 56.

29. P.L. 104-208. Illegal Immigration Reform and Immigrant Responsibility Act. §201-205. 30 September 1996.

30. P.L. 104-208. Illegal Immigration Reform and Immigrant Responsibility Act. §211-212. 30 September 1996.

In February 2003, four employees, including a visa adjudicator, from the U.S. Consulate in Nuevo Laredo, Mexico were indicted on charges of selling visas to people who may not have been eligible to receive one.[31] Working with outside conspirators, they sold United States visas for up to $1,500. The visa adjudicator, convicted under violations of IIRIRA, was sentenced to eighteen months in prison for his role in the sale of visas.[32] Similarly, just months after the incident in Mexico, a lawyer and his wife pled guilty to conspiracy for their role in a visa fraud scheme bringing Chinese immigrants into the United States. Two officials from National American University were also charged.[33]

An increase in penalties for immigration violations is a common theme throughout IIRIRA. In addition to consequences for providing illegal aliens with false documentation, penalties have intensified for foreign nationals who may have entered the United States legally. IIRIRA imposed a series of bars to admissibility for those who have overstayed in the U.S., as well as for those who have previously been deported. Upon entry to the U.S., nonimmigrants are issued a card (known as an I-94 card) that states the status under which the alien entered the U.S. and when that status expires. After the expiration date listed on the I-94, if the alien is still residing in the U.S., unlawful presence begins to accrue. International students are an exception; their cards do not have a specific expiration date. Rather, their I-94 cards state "D/S"— duration of status — meaning that so long as the students maintain the requirement of a student visa they are eligible to remain in the United States. Unlawful presence for international students can only be accrued upon declaration of an immigration judge. Should the nonimmigrant leave the United States after accruing more than

---

31. "News Release: Consular Employee in Nuevo Laredo, Mexico Charged with Conspiracy to Commit Visa Fraud." U.S. Department of Justice. Washington, 5 February 2003.

32. Zarazua, Jeorge. "Visa Dealers Sentenced to Federal Prison." *San Antonio Express News.* 26 July 2003.

33. Siskind, Gregory. "Siskin's Immigration Bulletin." ‹http://www.visalaw.com/02dec2/7dec202.html›. 13 December 2002.

180 days of unlawful presence, that foreign national would be subject to the three-year bar.[34] Moreover, those unlawfully present for more than one year are subject to a ten-year bar.

It becomes particularly problematic when an alien is ordered to be deported, but its country refuses to allow the alien to return. The Supreme Court ruled on *Zadvydas* v. *Davis* in June 2001, stating that an alien cannot be held indefinitely even if no other country will accept the deported individual. The court concluded, "Once removal is no longer reasonably foreseeable, continued detention is no longer authorized by the statute."[35] With this ruling the INS, just months before 9/11, was forced to release over three thousand aliens from custody. The majority were from Cuba, Vietnam, Cambodia, or Laos.[36] The Court, however, did provide an exception, which became important after 9/11. It stated, "The provision authorizing detention does not apply narrowly to 'a small segment of particularly dangerous individuals,' Hendricks, supra, at 368, say, suspected terrorists, but broadly to aliens ordered removed for many and various reasons, including tourist visa violations."[37] This distinction has been part of the justification for holding aliens indefinitely after the terrorist attacks of September 11.

Much of the controversy surrounding IIRIRA had to do with its expanded grounds for removal. With IIRIRA, expedited removal was introduced as a means to deport inadmissible aliens. Unlike deportation prior to IIRIRA, expedited removal allows the U.S. government to remove someone from the United States without a hearing. If someone is found at a point of entry to be inadmissible because of improper documentation or prior bars to admissibility, among other reasons, he can be immediately deported. As also specified under IIRIRA, the General Accounting Office was

---

34. P.L. 104-208. Illegal Immigration Reform and Immigrant Responsibility Act. §301. 30 September 1996.

35. *Zadvydas* v. *Davis*. 533 U.S. 678. 28 June 2001.

36. Frieden, Terry. "U.S. Ponders Release of Criminal Aliens." CNN News. ‹http://archives.cnn.com/2001/LAW/ 07/19/ashcroft.ins.detaine/index.html›. 19 July 2001.

37. Zadvydas v. Davis. 533 U.S. 678. 28 June 2001.

required to complete a study on the expedited removal process. That study, released in 2000, explained the steps involved in removing an alien expeditiously:[38]

- Explain the expedited removal process to the alien and read the statement of rights and consequences in a language the alien can understand. Included in this statement are the facts that the alien may be immediately removed from this country without a hearing and, if so, may be barred from reentering the country for 5 years or longer; that this may be the alien's only opportunity to present information to the inspector before INS makes a decision; and that if the alien has a fear or concern about being removed from the United States or being sent to his or her home country, the alien should tell the inspector during this interview because the alien may not have another chance to do so.

- Take a sworn statement from the alien, which is to contain all pertinent facts of the case. As part of the sworn statement process, the inspector provides information to the alien, interviews the alien, and records the alien's responses. The inspector is to cover and document in the sworn statement topics such as the alien's identity and reasons for the alien being inadmissible into the United States; whether the alien has a fear of persecution or torture or return to his or her home country; and the INS decision (i.e., issue the alien an expedited removal order, refer the alien for a credible fear interview, permit the alien to withdraw his or her application for admission, admit the alien into the country, allow him or her to apply for any applicable waiver, or defer the inspection or otherwise parole the alien). When the inspector completes the record of the sworn statement, he or she is to have the alien read the statement, or have it read to the alien, and have the alien sign and initial each page of the statement and any corrections that are made. The inspector is to provide a copy of the signed statement to the alien. The alien is to be given an opportunity to respond to INS' decision.

- Complete other administrative processes and paperwork, including the documents needed to remove the alien.

- Present the sworn statement and all other related paperwork to the appropriate supervisor for review and approval.

---

38. "Improve Expedited Removal Process." GAO/GGD-00-176. General Accounting Office. Washington: GPO: September 2000.

Expedited removal, as a tool to protect the country, is used to prevent the possibility of a noncitizen who has been ordered removed from slipping through the cracks and failing to appear for a removal hearing. The same GAO also discussed the percentage of aliens asking for asylum (those seeking asylum are exempt from expedited deportation without an asylum hearing) who were ordered removed but not detained; many failed to show up for their deportation hearings. The study cited, "GAO's analysis of data on aliens who were found to have a credible fear of persecution or torture between April 1, 1997, and September 30, 1999, showed that 2,351 aliens were released and had received an immigration judge's decision. Of the 2,351 aliens, 1,000 (or 42 percent) of them had not appeared for their removal hearings. In all 1,000 cases in which aliens did not appear for their removal hearings, immigration judges ordered them removed from the United States *in absentia*."[39] Obviously, a 42% rate of failure to appear is alarming and raises questions regarding the potential for a threat to the safety of the country, particularly since a similar study conducted by the Department of Justice's Office of the Inspector General reported that only about 11% of those who were not detained prior to their hearing were actually deported if so ordered.[40]

The number of those eligible to be detained greatly increased under IIRIRA. This was partly due to the IIRIRA expanding the distinction between criminal penalties and immigration penalties; what may have minor criminal implications may also have hefty immigration consequences for both nonimmigrants and legal permanent residents. Prior to IIRIRA, a criminal noncitizen would be reviewed to determine if the individual was deportable and if that person should indeed be removed.[41]

---

39. *Ibid.*

40. Department of Justice, Office of Inspector General Inspection Report, Immigration and Naturalization Service. Deportation of Aliens After Final Orders Have Been Issued (I-96-03, Mar. 1996).

With criminal convictions, IIRIRA expanded the definition, for immigration purposes, of what constitutes an aggravated felony. Should a noncitizen be convicted of an aggravated felony, after the completion of a criminal sentence, immigration officials can now detain the individual until the removal hearing. Noncitizens would have incentive not to return to their removal hearing because under IIRIRA, any order for removal due to an aggravated felony constitutes a lifetime bar to reentry. This provision has also been the source of much debate, particularly since it was retroactive covering any crimes committed after November 18, 1988. A case in 2003, *Demore v. Kim*, was forwarded to the Supreme Court to determine if a legal permanent resident can and should be held by immigration pending a removal hearing. Hyung Joon Kim, a permanent resident of the U.S., committed a burglary and upon release was detained by the INS without the option for bail. Kim argued that the denial of bail was unconstitutional and violated his right to due process.[42] Justice Sandra Day O'Connor cited in her comments §303(e) of IIRIRA, which states: "The Attorney General's discretionary judgment regarding the application of this section shall not be subject to review. No court may set aside any action or decision by the Attorney General under this section regarding the detention or release of any alien or the grant, revocation, or denial of bond or parole."[43]

Understandably, given the absolute nature of §303(e), the Supreme Court justices were deeply divided in the case with a 5-4 decision. In his dissent, Justice David H. Souter affirmed, "The Court's holding that the Due Process Clause allows this under a blanket rule is devoid of even ostensible justification in fact and at odds with the settled standard of liberty."[44] It remains a delicate

---

41. Morawetz, Nancy. "Understanding the Impact of the 1996 Deportation Laws and the Limited Scope of Proposed Reforms." *Harvard Law Review.* 113(8), 2000.

42. No. 01-1491. *Demore v. Kim.* U.S. Supreme Court. 29 April 2003.

43. P.L. 104-208. Illegal Immigration Reform and Immigrant Responsibility Act. §303(e). 30 September 1996.

44. No. 01-1491. *Demore v. Kim.* 29 April 2003.

situation; a noncitizen can be held with few options to challenge the detention, an element of IIRIRA that has been used to the government's advantage in fighting the war on terrorism, often to the detriment of the noncitizens being held — most of whom are not terrorists. As Nancy Morawetz makes clear in an article written for the *Harvard Law Review*, "Reforming the new mandatory deportation rules ... is central to any solution. Unless individuals are provided with a forum to present their cases to remain in this country, it will be difficult to control governmental efforts to maximize the yield of 'criminal aliens' deported."[45]

This ruling is different from an earlier yet equally important ruling, *INS v. St. Cyr*, in which the court ruled that judicial courts (as opposed to administrative courts, of which immigration court would be an example)[46] do have authority over questions of legality and constitutionality of immigration laws. Decided in June 2001, this case contends that courts can review a question of law unless Congress made clear its intentions not to allow for judicial review. The court ruled:[47]

> The INS also makes a separate argument based on 8 U. S. C. §1252(b)(9) (1994 ed., Supp. V). We have previously described §1252(b)(9) as a "zipper clause." *Reno v. American-Arab Anti-Discrimination Committee*, 525 U. S. 471, 483 (1999). Its purpose is to consolidate "judicial review" of immigration proceedings into one action in the court of appeals, but it applies only "[w]ith respect to review of an order of removal under subsection (a)(1)." 8 U. S. C. §1252(b) (1994 ed., Supp. V).37 Accordingly, this provision, by its own terms, does not bar habeas jurisdiction over removal orders not subject to judicial review under §1252(a)(1) including orders against aliens who are removable by reason of having committed one or more criminal offenses. Subsection (b)(9) simply provides for the consolidation of issues to be brought in petitions for "[j]udicial review," which, as we note above, is a term historically distinct from habeas. See Mahadeo v. Reno, 226 F. 3d 3, 12 (CA1

45. Morawetz, Nancy. "Understanding the Impact of the 1996 Deportation Laws and the Limited Scope of Proposed Reforms." *Harvard Law Review*. 113(8), 2000.

46. 533 U. S. 289, 308– 309. *INS v. St. Cyr*. 2001.

47. No. 00-767. *INS v. St. Cyr*. U.S. Supreme Court. 25 June 2001.

2000); *Flores-Miramontes v. INS*, 212 F. 3d 1133, 1140 (CA9 2000). It follows that §1252(b)(9) does not clearly apply to actions brought pursuant to the general habeas statute, and thus cannot repeal that statute either in part or in whole.

If it were clear that the question of law could be answered in another judicial forum, it might be permissible to accept the INS' reading of §1252. But the absence of such a forum, coupled with the lack of a clear, unambiguous, and express statement of congressional intent to preclude judicial consideration on habeas of such an important question of law, strongly counsels against adopting a construction that would raise serious constitutional questions. 38 Cf. Felker, 518 U. S., at 660-661. Accordingly, we conclude that habeas jurisdiction under §2241 was not repealed by AEDPA and IIRIRA.

IIRIRA also worked to improve the Visa Waiver Program (VWP). This program allows citizens of twenty-seven countries, mostly Western European nations, to enter the United States as a tourists without visas. This is a reciprocal program, meaning that U.S. citizens need not obtain a tourist visa for entry into the program's participating countries. Post 9/11, the VWP has come under fire, most notably because terrorist Richard Reid, the shoe bomber, held a British passport and thus he did not require a visa; the process of applying for a visa would have entailed additional security reviews. Section 635 of IIRIRA requires reporting of the percentage of those from VWP participating countries who have overstayed the period allotted under the VWP. A country which has more than a two percent rate of violations among its citizens entering the U.S. under the VWP will be put on probation and can potentially be disqualified from the program. Yet, a report conducted by the Department of Homeland Security's Office of the Inspector General in regard to these statistics on "disqualification rates" found that:[48]

---

48. Ervin, Clark Kent. "An Evaluation of the Security Implications of the Visa Waiver Program." DHS Office of Inspector General. ‹http://www.dhs.gov/dhspublic/interweb/assetlibrary/ OIG_SecurityImpVisaWaiverProg Eval_Apr04.pdf›. April 2004.

We were unable to confirm that DHS submitted required VWP overstay reports. The Illegal Immigration Reform and Immigrant Responsibility Act (IIRIRA) of 1996 requires annual reporting on the number of VWP visitors "for whom no matching departure record has been obtained...with an accounting by the alien's country of nationality and date of arrival in the U.S." Without these reports, the government cannot accurately evaluate the potential risks to U.S. security posed by a country's continued participation in the VWP.

We asked several officials whether any such reports had been submitted, but did not receive clear responses. One official suggested that we ask the congressional liaison office of the former INS, an office that no longer exists. A former INS official said that reports were not submitted and that INS did not have adequate information or records to complete the reports.

After 9/11 there was much discussion regarding the elimination of the VWP because of the ease with which potential terrorists can enter the U.S., but no action was taken. Shortly after the terrorist attacks, Congress did enact the Uniting and Strengthening America by Providing Appropriate Tools Required to Intercept and Obstruct Terrorism Act of 2001 (USA PATRIOT Act). Though the majority of the act greatly affected American citizens, some provisions in the USA PATRIOT Act are directed, not surprisingly, at foreign nationals.

The Act opens by stating that, "Arab Americans, Muslim Americans, and Americans from South Asia play a vital role in our Nation and are entitled to nothing less than the full rights of every American."[49] While the words of the §102 of the USA PATRIOT Act are clear, the actions of the United States government towards those who are entitled to the "full rights of every American" remain, in some instances, contradictory to this proclamation. This debate has received considerable media attention in the case of Jose Padilla, a U.S.-born citizen, who is accused of conspiring with al-Qaeda to

---

49. HR 3162 RDS. USA PATRIOT Act. §102. 24 October 2001.

plan terrorist attacks against the country. Declared an "enemy combatant" by the Attorney General, he is now afforded fewer rights than other American citizens, raising questions about civil liberties and constitutional rights.[50]

The term "enemy combatant" was first defined in 1942 in the case of *Ex Parte Quirin*, in which Nazis entered U.S. territory in a submarine. One defendant in this case was a U.S. citizen. They were not considered prisoners of war, but rather combatants. Like Padilla, they went before a military tribunal, could be held indefinitely, and could be interrogated more aggressively than American citizens criminally charged.[51] With regard to the U.S. citizen in the *Ex Parte Quirin* case, the court found that "The Government, however, takes the position that on attaining his majority he elected to maintain German allegiance and citizenship or in any case that he has by his conduct renounced or abandoned his United States citizenship."[52] Jose Padilla is treated on the basis of the same rationale. The conditions under which one may lose citizenship are clearly stated in all U.S. passports.

The USA PATRIOT Act does, however, mandate that anyone suspected of terrorism is to be held in custody until he can be removed from the U.S. The Act requires that removal proceedings or criminal charges be brought within seven days of capture. This is different from the treatment prescribed for those who are declared enemy combatants because, unlike enemy combatants, those to whom $412 applies will be subject to administrative or criminal proceedings rather than military.[53] In most cases, however, it is highly unlikely that the Attorney General would be in an urgent rush to have any terrorism suspect deported shortly after capture. Therefore, the person will be declared an enemy of the state so that

---

50. "Dirty Bomb Suspect Has Fewer Legal Rights." CNN News. ‹http://archives.cnn.com/2002/ LAW/06/11/prisoner.status/index.html›. 11 June 2002.

51. *Ibid.*

52. 317 U.S. 1 87 L.Ed.7. Ex Parte Quirin. U.S. Supreme Court. 1942.

53. HR 3162 RDS. USA PATRIOT Act. $412. 24 October 2001.

he can be detained and interrogated for additional intelligence information.

Under the USA PATRIOT Act, citizens and noncitizens alike saw their rights limited. Paragraph §326 of the Act requires financial institutions to confirm the identity of anyone opening an account and to check that information against terrorist lists provided by the government. Furthermore, is also required banks to complete a report for submission to the government showing how they will collect this information from foreign nationals with holdings at their bank.[54]

The USA PATRIOT Act requires the sharing of information with the government. The Act also allows for more interdepartmental information sharing. Section 203 allows for information obtained in criminal investigations to be shared with immigration officials when that information involves foreign intelligence data. Foreign intelligence information is defined as:

(I) information, whether or not concerning a United States person, that relates to the ability of the United States to protect against—

(aa) actual or potential attack or other grave hostile acts of a foreign power or an agent of a foreign power; or

(bb) sabotage or international terrorism by a foreign power or an agent of a foreign power; or

(cc) clandestine intelligence activities by an intelligence service or network of a foreign power or by an agent of foreign power; or

(II) information, whether or not concerning a United States person, with respect to a foreign power or foreign territory that relates to—

(aa) the national defense or the security of the United States; or

(bb) the conduct of the foreign affairs of the United States.

In addition to information sharing among domestic entities, the USA PATRIOT Act allows for the Department of State to share

---

54. HR 3162 RDS. USA PATRIOT Act. §326. 24 October 2001.

information contained in its visa lookout database with foreign governments "on the basis of reciprocity."[55] This type of information exchange raises two points, first, because §413 requires reciprocity on the part of the foreign government, it is a provision that probably holds more weight for American investigators in obtaining information about foreign nationals suspected of terrorism. Second, this provision is problematic because it is unknown why a foreign government would need such information as that found in the consular's lookout database. The United States has no jurisdiction over how that information will be used in the hands of foreign governments and it creates an atmosphere of mistrust and potential danger for the immigrant. The majority of those applying for visas to come to the U.S. are not terrorists and, in the case of a scholar obtaining a work visa or someone intending to immigrate to the U.S., foreign governments may look unfavorably upon the decision to apply for a visa and might potentially hinder the person from leaving the home country.

Several aspects of the USA PATRIOT Act address the issue of protecting the U.S. borders. Section 402 authorizes the increase in the number of agents patrolling the northern border of the U.S. This section of the act triples the number of immigration agents at the northern border and allots an additional $50 million to improve the technology used in monitoring the northern border.[56] It is understandable that more officials would be needed to patrol the northern border because the rural landscape of much of the area makes it easy for an unwanted guest to slip into the U.S.; however, the majority of illegal immigrants enter the U.S. via the southern border. This is well known, and indeed the majority of the INS initiatives to deter illegal immigration throughout the 1990s occurred along the U.S.-Mexican border with operations taking place in El Paso, Texas, San Diego, California, El Centro, California, and Tucson, Arizona.[57]

---

55. HR 3162 RDS. USA PATRIOT Act. §413. 24 October 2001.
56. HR 3162 RDS. USA PATRIOT Act. §402. 24 October 2001.

Considerable attention was given in the USA PATRIOT Act to expanding the INS's power, in part by allowing the INS and the Department of State, responsible for the issuance of visas, to access the FBI's National Crime Information Center's Interstate Identification Index (NCIC-III), the Wanted Persons File, and other files within the National Crime Information Center.[58] Such information as specified in §403 always should have been accessible to immigration officials and consular officers. Even before 9/11, it would have been reasonable to verify whether those applying for visas to enter the U.S. had a criminal background or were on a "wanted person" list. Furthermore, §405 asks the Attorney General to determine the "feasibility of enhancing the Integrated Automated Fingerprint Identification System (IAFIS) of the Federal Bureau of Investigation and other identification systems in order to better identify a person who holds a foreign passport or visa." Congress allotted "not less than" $2 million to complete this task.[59] In an era in which there were four attacks on U.S. entities in less than ten years (the 1993 WTC bombing, the embassy bombings in Tanzania and Kenya, and the bombing of the U.S.S. Cole), one might think it would have been prudent to not only determine the "feasibility" of enhancing security systems but to go ahead and implement any necessary changes.

Several sections of the USA PATRIOT Act address components of earlier laws, such as those in IIRIRA. Section 110 of IIRIRA mandates the development of an entry/exit data collection system in which all nonimmigrants entering or exiting the U.S. are required to have biometric information collected, i.e. fingerprints and a photograph. While IIRIRA gave the attorney general two years to create such a system, no specific date was given by which the system was to be fully implemented. Thus, it comes as no surprise that, prior to 9/11, no entry/exit system was fully

---

57. United States. "Yearbook of Immigration Statistics, 2003." U.S. Department of Homeland Security. Washington: GPO, 2004
58. HR 3162 RDS. USA PATRIOT Act. §403. 24 October 2001.
59. HR 3162 RDS. USA PATRIOT Act. §405. 24 October 2001.

operational. Though the USA PATRIOT Act made mention of this system, what is now known as US-VISIT, it too did not require a specific implementation date. The Act simply stated that such a system is to be implemented "with all deliberate speed and as expeditiously as practicable."[60]

In §416, the USA PATRIOT Act requires that a database tracking international students, as mandated under IIRIRA §641, be fully implemented by January 1, 2003. Unlike the US-VISIT system, a system to track foreign students was implemented (at least partially) before 9/11. The pilot program, Coordinated Interagency Partnership Regulating International Students (CIPRIS), was implemented two years after IIRIRA and discussion of the Student and Exchange Visitor Information System (SEVIS), the database that would permanently replace CIPRIS, was well established months before 9/11.[61]

The USA PATRIOT Act was one of the first steps taken after the watershed of 9/11 to try to better protect the United States from terrorist attacks. A second major step was to create the Department of Homeland Security (DHS). It is not often that a president is able to create a new cabinet-level department; it was last done with the Department of Veterans Affairs in 1989.[62] The creation of the Department of Homeland Security was the biggest governmental restructuring since the creation of the Department of Defense in 1947.[63] DHS joined the executive branch of the federal government on January 1, 2003.

The creation of this department is important from an immigration perspective because most immigration responsibilities under the INS were moved from the Department of Justice to DHS. The idea of drastically reforming and restructuring the INS was

---

60. HR 3162 RDS. USA PATRIOT Act. §414. 24 October 2001.

61. Cronin, Michael. Memo July 20, 2001.

62. "Facts about the Department of Veterans Affairs." U.S. Department of Veterans Affairs. ‹http://www1.va.gov/opa/fact/docs/vafacts.htm›. April 2003.

63. "Bush Signs Homeland Security Bill." CNN News. ‹http://archives.cnn.com/ 2002/ ALLPOLITICS/ 11/25/homeland.security/index.html›. 26 November 2002.

much discussed long before the creation of DHS. The Department of Justice issued a forty-two page restructuring proposal in November 2001, undoubtedly partly due to the negative attention the agency received post-9/11. This proposal included restructuring that would improve enforcement capabilities, create a clear chain of command and authority in an effort to improve accountability, enhance technology and security measures, and promote better customer service including timely processing, among other objectives.[64]

While many of these restructuring goals appear to be commonsense tactics that should have been implemented long ago, it is important to consider some of the outside forces influencing the INS. Illegal immigration increased dramatically throughout the 1990s, while funding, at least during the first half of the 1990s did not, forcing the INS to spread resources thin.[65] This is not to say, however, that there were not structural problems within the agency as well. As discussed more thoroughly in the next chapter, the INS has long suffered from having antiquated technology and a weak managerial structure, factors which contributed to many of the problems the agency had faced in the past.[66]

Originally, the revamping of the INS included dividing the agency into two separate bureaus, one for services, benefits, and adjudications and the other for enforcement, which would include border and customs enforcement. This separation was due in part to the conflicting nature of enforcement and service. As Former Attorney General John Ashcroft stated, "It is time to separate fully our service to legal immigrants who help build America ... from our enforcement against illegal aliens who violate the laws of America."[67]

---

64. "Immigration and Naturalization Service Restructuring Proposal." U.S. Department of Justice. Washington: GPO, 14 November 2001.

65. *Ibid.*

66. GAO-02-168T. "Immigration and Naturalization Service Overview of Recurring Management Challenges" General Accounting Office. Washington: GPO, 17 October 2001.

67. "Ashcroft Back House Bill to Split up INS." CNN News. ‹http://archives.cnn.com/ 2002/LAW/04/25/ ins.ashcroft/index.html›. 25 April 2002.

According to the restructuring proposal released by the Department of Justice, the new INS was to be ordered as follows:[68]

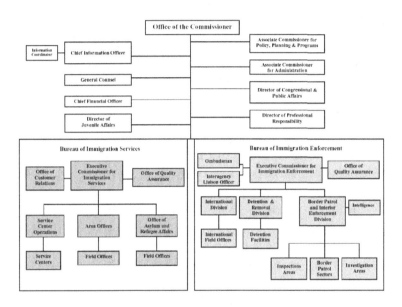

This restructuring proposal went before the House in April 2002 as the "Barbara Jordan Immigration Reform and Accountability Act," H.R. 3231, just months before it was reshaped as part of the Homeland Security Act. A letter signed by Judiciary Committee members James Sensenbrenner, Jr. and John Conyers, Jr. as well as members of the Subcommittee on Immigration and Claims George W. Gekas and Sheila Jackson Lee urged Congressional support for the bill, saying:[69]

---

68. "Immigration and Naturalization Service Restructuring Proposal." U.S. Department of Justice. Washington: 14 November 2001.

69. Sensenbrenner, F. James, et. al. Letter. "Support H.R. 3231, 'Barbara Jordan Immigration Reform and Accountability Act' to Overhaul the Immigration and Naturalization Service." 23 April 2002.

The need for overhauling the INS is undeniable. Americans regularly hear of the agency's latest blunder and observe an agency stumbling from one crisis to the next, with no coherent strategy of how to accomplish its missions. Consider these facts about the performance of today's INS: a backlog of 5 million unadjudicated petitions for immigration benefits force foreign nationals trying to play by the rules to wait in limbo for years. Furthermore, most of the several million undocumented foreign nationals are likely to never be deported. At least 300,000 foreign nationals ordered removed by immigration judges have absconded and cannot be found by the INS.

This same letter claims that the problems inherent in the INS are less about financial issues and more about "mission overload" in the conflicting duties required by the agency.[70]

On March 1, 2003, the INS was officially divided, though not as proposed in H.R. 3231. Under the Homeland Security Act, the INS was instead divided into three bureaus, one for services now known as the U.S. Citizenship and Immigration Services (USCIS), one for internal enforcement, Investigations and Customs Enforcement (ICE), and one for border and customs duties, Customs and Border Protection (CBP). These responsibilities, originally assumed by one agency, would now be split apart and would come under the new Department of Homeland Security.

In a different context it would be a feasible option not to put all of these agencies under DHS; however, in the wake of September 11, it is understandable that immigrants would be viewed as a threat and the agencies responsible for immigrant services and enforcement placed under DHS. Though the rationale for such a placement is understood, this does not imply that it is correct. Enforcement and customs and border protection do have a place in DHS, but the services sector does not. Placing USCIS with DHS makes the assumption that immigrants are inherently dangerous

---

70. *Ibid.*

and threatening, and that adjudicating immigration benefits is, in itself, a security matter.

The Homeland Security Act made still one more important distinction. Under this Act, it transferred the authority to make decisions regarding visa issuance from the Department of State to the Department of Homeland Security, though the Department of State would still be responsible for the day-to-day operation of visa issuance at its consulates and embassies.[71] CNN News reported that former Secretary of State Colin Powell was upset over this new delegation of authority, saying that, "Secretary of State Colin Powell reacted angrily to a proposal to strip his department of its power over visa applications and give it to the proposed Department of Homeland Security."[72]

Immigration law has indeed undergone various changes in the past decade. Although many of these laws were created in an effort to provide better protection from terrorist activities, it remains to be seen if these laws will produce their intended results. What is presently known, however, is that the United States, a country with a long history of welcoming immigrants, has slowly begun to close its doors by implementing stricter immigration controls in the name of security.

Failure to recognize the benefits of immigration and the fact that the vast majority of those who come to the U.S. are not terrorists, as well as failure to realize that terrorists need not be foreign, would result in an economic, political, and cultural loss for the whole country.

---

71. HR 5005. Homeland Security Act. §403. 23 January 2002.

72. Malveaux, Suzanne and Elise Labott. "Official: Powell Angry Over Visa Plan." CNN News. ‹http://archives.cnn.com/2002/ALLPOLITICS/06/17/homeland.defense.powell/index.html›. 17 June 2002.

3. THE IMPACT OF SEPTEMBER 11

"The terrorism attacks of September the eleventh underscore in the most painful way for Americans that we need better control over individuals coming to our shore from other nations."[1] Since 9/11, as Former Attorney General John Ashcroft made clear in his statement, the priority of the United States government and the agencies that control immigration in this country, now largely managed by the Customs and Border Protection (CBP), Citizenship and Immigration Services (CIS), and Investigations and Customs Enforcement (ICE), is protection.

The events of September 11 did not just happen. A combination of circumstances and inadequacies contributed to the tragedy. One of the agencies that came under scrutiny after the attack was the INS, since all the hijackers were foreign nationals. As the agency is responsible for overseeing the entry of nearly a half-billion[2] people into the United States each year, there is a strong possibility that some entrants might not receive the full attention they should;

---

1. Ashcroft, John. *INS Restructuring Plan.* U.S. Department of Justice. 14 November 2001.

2. 9/11 Commission. *9/11 Commission Report.* Washington: GPO, 2004.

however, management issues and system inadequacies greatly increased the likelihood that such oversights would occur.

The INS' management problems were well documented in a series of reports from the General Accounting Office (GAO), the National Academy of Public Administration,[3] and the National Performance Review, all of which issued reports on the "management challenges"[4] the INS had been experiencing for several years. At a hearing before the House of Representatives on the management practices of the Immigration and Naturalization Service, Associate Director of Administration of Justice Issues, General Governing Division, Laurie E. Ekstrand outlined five recurring problems within the INS including a lack of vision, untimely processing of applications, disorganized budget-development processes, "inadequate alien information systems," and a decentralized organizational structure.[5]

"Segmented management" and a disorganized budget processing system have been large contributors to the INS' problems in the past. A 1991 report by the GAO stated, "Compounding this lack of overall direction is a chaotic budget development process that has produced budgets that are simply complications of program submissions with little accountability for funds or attention to agencywide priorities."[6] The report called the financial record keeping of the INS "deplorable."[7] Furthermore, the poor managerial structure of the agency contributed not only to the budgetary chaos, but also to extreme mismanagement and inefficiency. Flaws in the administration throughout the 1980s and

---

3. "Managerial Options for the Immigration and Naturalization Service." National Academy of Public Administration. February 1991.

4. "Immigration and Naturalization Service Overview of Recurring Management Challenges." GAO-02-168T. General Accounting Office. Washington: GPO, 17 October 2001.

5. "Management Practices of the Immigration and Naturalization Service." Hearing Before the Subcommittee on Immigration and Claims of the Committee on the Judiciary House of Representatives. 8 February 1995.

6. "Immigration Management Strong Leadership and Management Reforms Needed to Address Serious Problems." GAO/GGD-91-28. General Accounting Office. Washington: GPO, January 1991.

7. *Ibid.*

1990s included a lack of leadership in enforcement procedures, poor organizational arrangement of the agency, and a lack of management oversight.[8] The 1995 hearing before the House reiterated some of these ongoing problems within the INS but qualified them by saying, "INS management problems did not develop overnight and they will not be solved overnight."[9] While an October 2001 report (also by the GAO) stated that improvements had been made in the prior decade, problems persisted.

In an effort to address some of these issues, the INS released a document in 1995 entitled "Strategic Plan: Towards INS 2000: Accepting the Challenge." One of the prominent features of this document is an explicit vision for the agency, something that was not clearly defined prior to this publication. This mission states:[10]

> The mission of the Service is to determine the admissibility of persons seeking entry and to adjust the status of and provide other benefits to legally entitled noncitizens within the country with proper regard for equity and due process. This includes assistance to those who seek permanent resident status and those who wish to become citizens through naturalization.
>
> It is the responsibility of the Service to ensure appropriate documentation of aliens at entry, to deny entry to those who are not legally admissible whether they attempt to enter through ports-of-entry or surreptitiously across the border, and to determine the status of those in the country. The Service is also responsible for deterring illegal entry and stay, including enforcement of criminal provisions against those who act or conspire to promote such entry and stay. Further, it is the responsibility of the Service to detect, apprehend, and remove those noncitizens whose entry was illegal, whether undocumented or fraudulent, and those found to have violated the conditions of their stay.

8. *Ibid.*

9. "Management Practices of the Immigration and Naturalization Service." Hearing Before the Subcommittee on Immigration and Claims of the Committee on the Judiciary House of Representatives. 8 February 1995.

10. United States. "Strategic Plan: Towards INS 2000: Accepting the Challenge." U.S. Immigration and Naturalization Service. Washington: GPO, 5 March 1995.

The twenty-six-page document outlines future goals for the agency and specifies objectives within those goals, and summarizes how these goals will be achieved. Aims include improvements in border control procedures, increased enforcement of immigration laws, reducing incentives to be in the United States illegally, services that are "timely, consistent, fair, and of high quality," a well-trained workforce, better management of resources, more structured leadership within the agency, and improvements in technology.[11] Though these are commendable objectives, there was a failure on the part of the INS and the U.S. government as a whole to recognize that these goals could not be achieved without cooperation and assistance from outside the agency.

One of the leading problems within the INS was lack of timely processing of applications. In the 1995 subcommittee hearing, it was stated that in some INS district offices it took ten months or more to process a naturalization application,[12] and while the USCIS now vows to have naturalization applications adjudicated in a year, other applications have considerably longer waiting periods. The inability for the INS to process applications in a timely manner has been and continues to be a problem for the USCIS, one of the three bureaus that were spun off under the Homeland Security Act. The demand to process applications quickly, however, has come at a price, as discussed in a 2001 GAO report stating, "Some adjudicators told us that because of pressure to adjudicate cases quickly, they did not routinely use investigations staff to look into potentially fraudulent applications because doing so would take more time and reduce the number of applications they could complete."[13]

However, the practice of adjudicating applications quickly, without proper review, was greatly disrupted with the release of the "Zero Tolerance" memorandum written by then INS commissioner

---

11. *Ibid.*

12. *Ibid.*

13. Stana, Richard M. "Immigration and Naturalization Services Overview of Recurring Management Challenges." General Accounting Office. GAO-02-168T. Washington: GPO, 17 October 2001.

James Ziglar in March 2002. Prompted by the failure of INS employees to follow protocol when they granted visa waivers to four Pakistanis who later went missing,[14] the memo stated that INS officials "who fail to abide by headquarters-issued policy and field guidance" would have their employment with the agency terminated.[15] While it is obvious that this memorandum was also related to the negative publicity the agency received regarding the change of status notifications that Mohammed Atta and Marwan Al-Shehhi received in March 2002, it is interesting that the leadership of the agency would take a stance of zero tolerance that is in direct contrast to the systematic practice of rewarding employees who adjudicate the most cases. Perhaps it would be a better management policy to reward adjudicators for completing application reviews in a thorough, correct manner rather than threatening them with termination of employment. A zero tolerance policy, as outlined in the memorandum, is a disservice not only to the employees of the INS but also to all the noncitizens who are applying for services from the INS, because in an effort to avoid the repercussions outlined in the June memorandum many cases will be denied without a complete and accurate review. Eventually the memo was rescinded, in September 2003; however, the "culture of no" that it created has had lasting effects throughout the adjudication process.[16]

The INS has had a long history of inefficiency. In addition to lengthy processing times for applications, communication and coordination within the agency has lacked competence. The 1995 subcommittee hearing gave several examples of the consultation and organization problems within the agency. Laurie Ekstrand of the GAO gave examples of this at the hearing,[17]

---

14. "INS in New Visa Row." CNN News. ⟨http://www.cnn.com/2002/US/03/23/ins.pakistanis/⟩. 23 March 2002.

15. Ziglar, James. "Zero Tolerance Memorandum." 19 March 2002.

16. Falstrom, Carl, Ed. "Countering the Culture of "No": Strategies for Business Immigration in 2004." American Immigration Lawyers Association. January 2004.

17. *Ibid.*

In February 1990, antismuggling agents from the Border Patrol office nearly arrested suspects who were the subject of Investigation's surveillance.

In June 1990, Border Patrol agents were involved in a fraud case that was directly related to an Investigation case.

In the above examples, the separate INS enforcement units were not aware of each other's cases.

Perhaps one of the most infamous examples of an INS mishap came in June 1999 when INS officials released serial killer Rafael Resendez-Ramirez, even though the agency had been notified by Texas law enforcement agents that he was suspected in several murders.

Part of what contributed to the release of Rafael Resendez-Ramirez was a lack of technology that would notify immigration agents of the danger Mr. Resendez-Ramirez posed to the country. Deputy Attorney General Eric Holder, stated, "There are a huge number of people who cross our borders every year, I mean it's in the millions and we want to try to make the system as complete as we possibly can. Part of this review will help us in that regard to determine what we don't have in the system that perhaps we need to have."[18]

Technological inadequacies have been a central problem for the INS. As far back as 1990, the General Accounting Office discussed the technological disadvantages of the agency. The report entitled "Information Management: The Immigration and Naturalization Service Lacks Ready Access to Essential Data" stated:[19]

> INS's manual and automated information systems are not giving top management and field staff the data needed to assess, monitor, and administer the Service's diverse and complex mission. According to INS executives and mid-level managers, the lack of

---

18. Thomas, Pierre. "INS Told About Murder Suspect, But Freed Him." CNN News.‹http://www.cnn.com/US/9907/ 01/ins.ramirez.02/index.html›. 1 July 1999

19. "Information Management: Immigration and Naturalization Service Lacks Ready Access to Essential Data." General Accounting Office. GAO/IMTEC-90-75. Washington: GPO, September 27, 1990.

reliable, timely, and complete information hinders their work and wastes scare resources.

In 2001, this point was reiterated by the GAO when it wrote in its report, "Effectively using information technology continues to remain a challenge for INS."[20]

According to former INS Commissioner Ziglar in testimony given before the House on March 19, 2002, the antiquated technology that the agency employed contributed to the slow processing times of applications as well as the incident of Huffman Aviation International receiving change of status approval notices for Atta and Al-Shehhi six months *after* the attacks of September 11. Commissioner Ziglar outlined the problems:[21]

> When I started this job about 7 months ago — one month before September 11 — I found that I inherited an information system, or more correctly, systems, that were big on information and small on technology. I found too much reliance on manual data entry, much of which had to be boxed and shipped to outside contractors. I found a lack of real-time data and a lack of readily accessible electronic information for accurate and timely reporting. I found that INS lacked interconnectivity among its own systems as well as with those of other law enforcement agencies, and found that enterprise architecture was still on the drawing board. I also found that the INS lacked a full-time Chief Information Officer who could be responsible for and analyze the best solutions to the agency's IT shortcomings. While some improvements have taken place in recent years, you and I both know that the pace of improvement has been well behind any reasonable definition of the Service's needs.

As one subcommittee member, Rep. Sheila Jackson Lee (D-Texas), pointed out in regards to the approval notice mishap, "We

---

20. "Immigration and Naturalization Service Overview of Recurring Management Challenges." General Accounting Office. GAO-02-168T. Washington: GPO, 17 October 2001.

21. Testimony of James W. Ziglar, Commissioner, Immigration and Naturalization Service, Before the House Committee on the Judiciary Subcommittee on Immigration Claims. 19 March 2002.

should be grateful this egregious error occurred with dead terrorists, not live ones."[22]

In the past, interagency communication had been a problem; however, the need to communicate and share information became even more apparent after the 9/11 attacks. Maura Harty, Assistant Secretary of the Department of State's Consular Affairs Office reported,[23]

> The Department of State, working with other agencies, has made significant improvements to our ability to share information — my colleagues here with me today represent institutions that symbolize this interagency commitment to information sharing. Thanks to this new level of collaboration, the data holdings in our consular lookout system now total 18 million records of people ineligible to receive visas, nearly triple what we had prior to September 11.

Though improvements have been made, loopholes in the immigration system continue to hinder other agencies from being notified of visa revocations or of the identity of individuals who may be a threat to the United States. This problem was outlined in the June 18, 2003 GAO report entitled, "Border Security: New Policies and Procedures Are Needed to Fill Gaps in the Visa Revocation Process." The report declared, "The visa revocation process broke down when information on individuals with revoked visas was not shared between State and appropriate immigration and law enforcement offices."[24] As *Federal Computer Weekly* also reported, "In theory, all intelligence agencies, including local law enforcement, should immediately be alerted when a visa is revoked on the grounds of terrorism."[25] Furthermore, as former INS Commissioner

---

22. *Ibid.*

23. Testimony of Maura Hartey, Assistant Secretary, Consular Affairs Office, Department of State. Before the 9/11 Commission. Seventh Hearing. 26 January 2004.

24. "Border Security: New Policies and Procedures Are Needed to Fill Gaps in the Visa Revocation Process." GAO-03-908T. General Accounting Office. Washington: GPO, 18 June 2003.

25. Reed, Margaret A.T. "Lawmakers Cite Visa Loopholes." *Federal Computer Weekly.* ‹http://www.fcw.com›. 19 June 2003.

Doris Meissner pointed out, "The immigration system can only set up gateways and tracking systems that exclude terrorists about whom the United States already has information, and/or enable authorities to find 'clean' operatives already in the country if new information is provided by intelligence agencies. The immigration and intelligence systems must work together for either to be effective."[26]

The INS and the current agencies that were formerly part of the INS were largely influenced by the politics surrounding immigration. The point was made by Janet A. Gilboy in an article written for *Law and Society Review* that political support for most governmental agencies comes from either the community, the executive branch, or the legislature and that the INS receives minimal support from the community and the executive branch of the government. This lack of support within the government combined with the fact that "an American ambivalence exists towards aliens in general and immigration enforcement in particular" creates an agency that is often an afterthought.[27] Many of the decisions that the INS makes are not popular decisions and garner little support outside the agency. As a consequence, the agency received limited funding prior to 9/11, and was at the will of the legislature, where there were few to lobby on its behalf, while other organizations and agencies do have the resources to lobby against the INS and to limit its power and influence. It is no wonder then that the INS evolved into an agency wrought with problems.

Interagency communication problems were not the only examples of communication difficulties encountered by the INS and other agencies and departments working with immigration. Some aspects of the adjudication process are outsourced to non-governmental agencies. A 2003 GAO report examined continued weaknesses such as having "not made good use of cross-functional

---

26. Testimony of Doris Meissner, Former Commissioner, Immigration and Naturalization Service. Before the 9/11 Commission. Seventh Hearing. 26 January 2004.

27. Gilboy, Janet A. "Penetrability of Administrative Systems: Political 'Casework' and Immigration Inspections." *Law & Society Review.* 26(2). 2001.

teams, resulting in poor coordination of contracting activities" between the legacy INS agency, ICE, and contracted companies.[28] While INS officials completed adjudications, notices of those adjudication results were often forwarded to an outside company who would then notify the applicant, and that information would be "entered into a database system and microfiched within five days, and returned to the school for its records after holding them 180 days."[29] The American public learned of this process six months to the day after September 11, when a flight school, Huffman Aviation International, received the change of status approval notices for hijackers Mohammed Atta and Marwan Al-Shehhi.[30]

Indeed, waiting for an answer to the form I-539 that was used to complete a change of nonimmigrant status did take several months — nineteen months from the time of filing, in the case of Atta and Al-Shehhi. Although the INS has vowed to expedite the processing of applications after September 11, aiming to make decisions on form I-539 within thirty days,[31] many school officials today will attest to the fact that that timeframe is inaccurate and ninety to one hundred twenty days is a more realistic number.[32] That is still an improvement from the processing times prior to the incident with Mohammed Atta and Marwan Al-Shehhi's change of status approval notices.

As outlined in a Justice Department report released on May 20, 2002, there was considerable mishandling of at least two of the 9/11 terrorists by the INS. Mohammed Atta, after applying for a change of status from visitor to student, and with an expired B visitor's visa,

---

28. Hardy, Michael. "GAO Raps INS on Contracting." *Federal Computer Weekly.* ‹http://www.fcw.com›. 25 August 2003.

29. Testimony of James W. Ziglar, Commissioner, Immigration and Naturalization Service, Before the House Committee on the Judiciary Subcommittee on Immigration Claims. 19 March 2002.

30. "INS Chief Blames Visa Mess on Old Technology." CNN News. ‹http://www.cnn.com/2002/ALLPOLITICS /03/19/ins.visa.mess/index.html›. 19 March 2002.

31. Testimony of James W. Ziglar, Commissioner, Immigration and Naturalization Service, Before the House Committee on the Judiciary Subcommittee on Immigration Claims. 19 March 2002.

32. NAFSA Listserve. 2004.

was allowed to leave the U.S. for a trip to Madrid and later reentered the U.S. to continue studying at a Florida flight school.[33] Not having a valid visa is reason enough to deny entry into the United States; however, when Mr. Atta produced an I-20 form he was allowed entry. An I-20, explained more thoroughly in the next chapter, is issued by a school and is used to assist in the attainment of a student visa and maintain nonimmigrant student status while in the U.S., however, the I-20 alone is not a visa nor is it alone sufficient for entry into the United States.[34]

The Point of Entry (POE) procedure requires individuals to undergo a primary inspection by an INS official upon disembarkment from the plane, though now with the INS divided, an official from the Customs and Border Protection (CBP) Agency completes this charge. Documents such as passports, visas, and any other pertinent immigration credentials are examined. During the inspection, the U.S. visa should be scanned or manually entered into a database known as the Interagency Border Information System (IBIS). IBIS is actually a compilation of a series of databases maintained by several government agencies such as the Department of State and the FBI among several other agencies.[35] If an alien's documents are not in order, or if IBIS shows an alert, the alien is then directed to secondary inspection. An officer conducting primary inspections does not have the authority to deny entry; this right is reserved for the officers of secondary inspection. On January 10, 2001, Mohammed Atta was granted entry into the United States after secondary inspection.

All nineteen of the terrorists of 9/11 initially entered the country legally. While some of them did fall out of status during their stay in the United States, all entered legally. To enter the United States legally, all of the hijackers had valid passports, although some were confirmed as fraudulent post-9/11. The

---

33. *Ibid.*

34. 8 CFR 214.

35. Fine, Glenn. "The Immigration and Naturalization's Contact with Two Terrorists." U.S. Department of Justice. Washington: GPO, 20 May 2002.

hijackers also needed a valid visa; and, depending on what kind of visa is used, supporting documentation, viz., an I-20 form if entering on a student visa, may also be required for entry.

Some foreign nationals from designated countries are allowed to enter the United States without a visa under the Visa Waiver Program (VWP); however, none of the hijackers qualified for a waiver because they were not nationals of participating countries. Former INS Commissioner Doris Meissner testified before the 9/11 Commission that, "Even under the best immigration controls, most of the September 11 terrorists would still be admitted to the United States today. That is because they had no criminal records, no known terrorist connections, and had not been identified by intelligence methods for special scrutiny."[36] The databases available to immigration officers at POEs against which to test arrivals in the United States were the TECS,[37] CIS-INS, and NAILS databases that checked names for terrorist connections, criminal records, or outstanding warrants.[38]

IMMIGRATION RELATED DATABASES

CCD — Consular Consolidated Database; provides information on previous visa applications and visa issuances

CLASS — Consular Lookout and Support System; used by consular offices to check visa applicants against a list that includes names of people who are known associates of terrorism

CIS-INS — Central Index System; provides history of immigrant contact with legacy INS or USCIS

---

36. Testimony of Doris Meissner, Former Commissioner, Immigration and Naturalization Service. Before the 9/11 Commission. Seventh Hearing. 26 January 2004.

37. CIBER Services. "U.S. Customs Service's (USCS) Treasury Enforcement Communications System Application Outsourcing." ‹http://www.ciber.com/index_var.cfm?pageid=/ services_solutions/fedgovt/main.cfm?id=fedgov-case-out-customs›. 2004.

38. Testimony of Jose E. Melendez-Perez, Inspector, Customs and Border Protection, Department of Homeland Security. Before the 9/11 Commission. 26 January 2004.

IBIS — Interagency Border Information System; database checked by consular officers when reviewing visa applications for issuance of a visa; this database consists of information from several databases including CLASS, SEVIS, NAILS, CLAIMS, and CCD

IDENT — Database maintained by DHS that includes fingerprint and other biometric information on foreign visitors to the United States

NAILS — National Automated Index Lookout System; lists foreign nationals who are not permitted into the U.S.

TECS — Treasury Enforcement Communication System; provides information regarding criminal history

The Visa Waiver Program (VWP) has been one of the most controversial systems post-9/11, because of its leniency in allowing nonimmigrants into the country. The VWP has always been a contentious program since its inception in the Immigration Reform and Control Act of 1986, but 9/11 has renewed the debate about the program. Those entering the U.S. under the VWP as visitors, a status that would normally require a B visa, are not obliged to obtain a visa. Currently, there are twenty-seven countries whose citizens are allowed to enter the U.S. for up to three months on the VWP. From 1998 to 2003, nearly 93 million nonimmigrants have entered the U.S. using the VWP.[39] The major concerns surrounding this program have in large part to do with the lack of consular pre-screening of the visitor (a process that would be completed if the individual were applying for a visa) and the possibility of stolen passports being used to gain easy entry into the country under the VWP.

A report from the DHS's Office of the Inspector General stated of the Visa Waiver Program that, "while VWP travelers in general

---

39. "An Evaluation of the Security Implications of the Visa Waiver Program." Department of Homeland Security Office of Inspector General. Washington: GPO, 26 April 2004.

are considered 'low risk' relative to those from countries not in VWP, there are sufficient problems with VWP travelers to constitute an added security risk."[40] This point has been reinforced by the fact that three known terrorists, Richard Reid, the al-Qaeda member who tried to deploy a bomb located in his shoes on an American Airlines flight in December 2001, Habib Zacarias Moussaoui, convicted of involvement in the 9/11 plot, and Ahmed Ajaj, convicted for his involvement in the 1993 WTC bombing, all entered the United States using the VWP.[41]

ACRONYMS OF IMMIGRATION PROGRAMS

NSEERS — National Security Entry/Exit Registration System; Registration system for males of twenty-five, mostly Middle Eastern countries, over the age of fourteen

US-VISIT — United States Visitor and Immigrant Status Indicator Technology; System implemented at consulates abroad and POEs requiring most visa holders to be photographed and fingerprinted and to complete exit procedures upon departure from the United States.

VWP — Central Index System; provides history of immigrant contact with legacy INS or USCIS

Dianne Feinstein (D-CA), a major opponent of the program, argued, "Post 9/11, security issues must trump other concerns. It is clear to me that the Visa Waiver Program is ripe for abuse. We must address these issues and ensure that terrorists cannot exploit these holes in our security."[42] Indeed the Visa Waiver Program raises serious security concerns for the United States. International students, in the wake of terrorist threats to the U.S., have been the

---

40. *Ibid.*

41. *Ibid.*

42. Feinstein, Dianne. "Senator Feinstein Seeks Major Improvements to the Visa Waiver Program." ‹http://feinstein.senate.gov›. 13 May 2004.

target of increased scrutiny. Though only one of the men implicated in the 1993 WTC bombing was a student, and six of the 9/11 terrorists had some connection to student nonimmigrant status, it is the VWP which has been utilized by at least 157 known terrorists.[43] Those 157 were the ones who were denied entry by immigration officials; how many others slipped through using the VWP?

Perhaps one of the biggest flaws of the Visa Waiver Program is the use of fraudulent passports from VWP participating countries in an effort to enter the United States. At a hearing before the House Committee on International Relations, DHS Inspector General Clark Ervin made the point, "The lost and stolen passport problem is the greatest security problem associated with the Visa Waiver Program. Our country is vulnerable because gaps in our treatment of lost and stolen passports remain."[44]

One step that has been taken in an effort to reduce passport fraud and to provide additional security measures for those participating in the VWP was the requirement to have machine-readable passports. Machine-readable passports comply with the standards of the International Civil Aviation Organization (ICAO) and include biographical data that can quickly be scanned by immigration officers. The compliance date for this feature was set as October 26, 2004, though some countries within the VWP met compliance in October 2003.[45] Originally, machine-readable passports were not required until 2007 under the Visa Waiver Permanent Program Act of 2000; however, the USA PATRIOT Act revised that date in an effort to make the United States more secure after 9/11.[46] Also, by October 26, 2005, participants of the VWP are

---

43. "An Evaluation of the Security Implications of the Visa Waiver Program." Department of Homeland Security Office of Inspector General. Washington: GPO, 26 April 2004.

44. Testimony of Clark Kent Ervin, Inspector General, United States Department of Homeland Security. Before the U.S. House of Representatives. 23 June 2004.

45. "Visa Waiver Program: Important Notices." ⟨http://travel.state.gov/visa/tempvisitors_novisa_waiver.html⟩. October 2004.

46. "Visa Waiver Program." Congressional Research Service Report for Congress. Washington: GPO, 6 April 2004.

required to have biometric passports, which includes a "biometric identifier"[47] to further enhance the security of the program, though this date has been extended on past occasions and may be extended again in 2005. Along with the urgings of the travel industry and the education community,[48] both the Department of Homeland Security and the Department of State[49] had asked Congress for a two-year extension to the original October 2004 deadline for biometric passports because "most countries are unable to meet the original October 2004 date to include biometrics in passports due to several technology-related reasons."[50] Without the deadline extension, as the OIG report states, "The Department of State is now facing what one official calls 'a train wreck' on October 27, 2004, the date when the VWP would become unavailable as a travel option for large numbers of travelers without biometric ICAO compliant passports."[51] The date of compliance for biometric passports has been extended and it remains to be seen if the Department of State will still be facing a "train wreck" in October 2005.

An improvement in the security of passports is only one step of many needed to make the VWP more secure. The DHS Inspector General's report makes fourteen recommendations for improving the program. In addition to improvements in the way passports are reviewed, improvements in management, completion of annual reports, and reviews of countries participating in the program were also recommended.[52]

---

47. Ibid.

48. NAFSA Listserve. "NAFSA Advocacy Action Alert." 21 July 2004.

49. "Departments of Homeland Security and State Request Extensions for Biometric Passport Requirement, Visa Waiver Program Travelers to be Enrolled in US-VISIT." Department of Homeland Security. Washington, 2 April 2004.

50. "Departments of Homeland Security and State Request Extensions for Biometric Passport Requirement, Visa Waiver Program Travelers to be Enrolled in US-VISIT." U.S. Department of Homeland Security. Washington, 2 April 2004.

51. United States. "An Evaluation of the Security Implications of the Visa Waiver Program." OIG-04-26. Department of Homeland Security Office of Inspector General. Washington: GPO, April 2004.

52. Ibid.

Had the 9/11 terrorists tried to enter under the VWP and had their documents been reviewed thoroughly and properly, the 9/11 Commission suggests, indicators were present that should have barred the hijackers from being allowed to enter the United States. There were indicators that would have prohibited them from being granted a visa, as well. The 9/11 Commission listed seven points. They:[53]

- Included among them known al-Qaeda operatives who could have been watchlisted;
- Presented passports 'manipulated in a fraudulent manner;
- Presented passports with "suspicious indicators" of extremism;
- Made detectable false statements on their visa applications;
- Were pulled out of the travel stream and given greater scrutiny by border officials;
- Made false statements to border officials to gain entry to the United States; and
- Violated immigration laws while inside the United States.

Knowing this information existed regarding several of the hijackers prior to 9/11, we come to the question of how these individuals could be allowed into the United States and why the immigration officials missed all the cues that would have alerted them to the potential danger that these people posed to this country. Evidence seems to suggest that the immigration officials, both the consular officers overseas who were responsible for the issuance of visas and the immigration officials at POEs in the U.S., did not violate the protocols of their profession; there simply were not safeguards in place for immigration officials to verify information or to recognize violations in immigration status.

Like Mohammed Atta and Marwan Al-Shehhi, Ziad Samir Jarrah entered the United States for the purpose of studying at a flight school, though all of them entered the United States as tourists, rather than as students. The Foreign Affairs Manual states:[54]

---

53. 9/11 Commission Staff Statement No. 4, Hearing 7. 27 January 2004.

9 FAM 41.11 N3.1 Principal Purpose of Admission

(TL:VISA-2; 08-30-1987)

An alien desiring to come to the United States for one principal, and one or more incidental, purposes should be classified in
accordance with the principal purpose. For example, the consular
officer should classify as F-1 or M-1 an alien seeking to enter the
United States as a student who desires, prior to entering an
approved school, to make a tourist trip of not more than 60 days
within the United States.

Unlike Atta and Al-Shehhi, Jarrah did not change his status to
that of a student; and while an individual is responsible for his/her
immigration status, it is also important to consider here what
responsibility the school has in a situation like this. It could be
argued that the school that enrolled him for full-time flight training
was partly at fault for allowing tourists to study full-time at their
facility, because his study at the flight school was the primary
reason for coming to this country and was not incidental to his stay
in the United States.

During the time when the hijackers applied for their visas, it
was standard procedure for applicants to submit visa applications
via the mail or through a third party such as an agent. Rarely were
tourist or student visa applicants required to be interviewed
personally by consular officials, unless there was a problem or
concern with the application. Most applications were denied on the
basis of failure to disprove immigrant intent[55] (which is the
reasoning given for most denials still today, though it is often likely
that a student is being denied on the basis of other concerns).
Christine Colburn, International Student Advisor at the
Massachusetts Institute of Technology, says, "The people who end
up getting denied were for immigrant intent; they went through the
whole security check and in the end they got denied for immigrant

---

54. Foreign Affairs Manual. 9 FAM 41.11 N3.1 Principal Purpose of Admission
55. 9/11 Commission Staff Statement No. 1 Hearing 7. 26 January 2004.

intent, that's always the fall-back position."[56] The nineteen hijackers of September 11 were able to overcome the "intent to immigrate" concerns that so often are the focus of consular officers, though four of their co-conspirators were not able to do so. Ramzi Binalshibh, Zakariya Essabar, Ali Abdul Aziz Ali, and Saeed al Gambi were all denied visas, not because they were perceived as terrorists, but rather because they could not disprove intent to immigrate to the United States.[57]

In an effort to obtain visas, the opportunity for fraud existed and was exploited by at least one of the terrorists. Prior to 9/11 biometric information was not required for visa issuance, with the exception of some visas issued to Mexican citizens, though it is now required under the US-VISIT system at all consulates and embassies.

This was a weakness in the visa issuance process that was exploited by a hijacker on United Airlines flight #175. As explained during the 9/11 Commission hearings:[58]

> With the exception of Mexico, biometric information — like a fingerprint — was not routinely collected from visa applicants before 9/11. Terrorists therefore easily could exploit opportunities for fraud. Khalid Sheikh Mohamed, the chief tactical planner and coordinator of the 9/11 attacks, was indicted in 1996 by Federal authorities in the Southern District of New York for his role in earlier terrorist plots. Yet KSM, as he is known, obtained a visa to visit the United States on July 23, 2001, about six weeks before the 9/11 attacks. Although he is not a Saudi citizen and we do not believe he was in Saudi Arabia at the time, he applied for a visa using a Saudi passport and an alias, Abdulrahman al Ghamdi. He had someone else submit his application and photo through the Visa Express program. There is no evidence that he ever used this visa to enter the United States.

Tools that could have been used to assist consular and immigration officers in determining the eligibility of visa

---

56. Interview with author. 2 June 2004.
57. 9/11 Commission Staff Statement No. 1 Hearing 7. 26 January 2004.
58. *Ibid.*

applications and noncitizens entering the country are now beginning to be implemented with mixed reactions from the American public. A system such as US-VISIT, which records biometric information, fingerprints and photos, is being implemented as part of an entry-exit system throughout the United States. The entry requirement was fully operational in September 2004. In theory, this system would aid immigration enforcement officials in preventing visa fraud, apprehending terrorists, and determining who has overstayed their visas. Additionally, machine-readable passports are required for all those entering the U.S., while programs such as SEVIS, a national data-tracking system of international students and exchange visitors, has already been fully implemented. Though these systems are designed to aid immigration officials, they alone will not deter or prevent terrorism unless they are fully utilized by the agencies.

One system that was implemented after 9/11 in an effort to deter terrorism was the National Security Entry/Exit Registration System (NSEERS). Beginning in November 2002,[59] groups of nonimmigrant males, mostly of Middle Eastern descent, residing in the United States and born in 1986 or earlier, were required to register at their local INS district offices.[60]

During the time period between December 16, 2002 and December 1, 2003, noncitizens of the countries listed below (among others) were required to register, at the discretion of the immigration officer, as they entered the United States. This created confusion because while all nonimmigrants of the listed countries present in the United States during the call-in period were required to register with the INS, not all males entering the U.S. from those countries were required to register. As stated in the initial

---

59. Federal Register. "Registration of Certain Nonimmigrant Aliens From Designated Countries; Notice." 6 November 2002.

60. Federal Register. "Registration of Certain Nonimmigrant Aliens From Designated Countries; Notice." 22 November 2002.

Federal Register. "Registration of Certain Nonimmigrant Aliens From Designated Countries; Notice." 6 December 2002.

Federal Register. "Registration of Certain Nonimmigrant Aliens From Designated Countries; Notice." 6 December 2002.

announcement of the NSEERS program in the November 6, 2002 Federal Register, "Based on intelligence information available to the Attorney General, the Attorney General has determined that registering all nonimmigrant aliens from the covered countries would not enhance security."[61] An immigration official at a POE could potentially require anyone to register; this was not limited to the twenty-five countries listed for the NSEERS call-in registration. Any person, male or female, from any country in the world, could be registered at the discretion of the immigration officer.

NSEERS REGISTRATION

	Call-in Group 1	Call-in Group 2	Call-in Group 3	Call-in Group 4
Registration	December 6, 2002	January 10, 2003	March 21, 2003	April 25, 2003
	Iran	Afghanistan	Pakistan	Bangladesh
	Iraq	Algeria	Saudi Arabia	Egypt
	Libya	Bahrain		Indonesia
	Sudan	Eritrea		Jordan
	Syria	Lebanon		Kuwait
		Morocco		
		North Korea		
		Oman		
		Qatar		
		Somalia		
		Tunisia		
		UAE		
		Yemen		

---

61. Federal Register. "Registration of Certain Nonimmigrant Aliens From Designated Countries; Notice." 16 December 2002.

The authority for NSEERS registration came under 8 CFR 264.1(f)(4). The law states:

f) Registration, fingerprinting, and photographing of certain nonimmigrants. (Paragraph (f) revised 12/2/03; 68 FR 67578); (Paragraph (f) revised effective 9/11/02; 67 FR 52584)

(4) Registration of aliens present in the United States.

(i) The Secretary of Homeland Security, by publication of a notice in the Federal Register, also may impose such special registration, fingerprinting, and photographing requirements upon nonimmigrant aliens who are nationals, citizens, or residents of specified countries or territories (or a designated subset of such nationals, citizens, or residents) who have already been admitted to the United States or who are otherwise in the United States. A notice under this paragraph (f)(4) shall explain the procedures for appearing in person and providing the information required by the Department of Homeland Security, providing fingerprints, photographs, or submitting supplemental information or documentation.

(ii) Any nonimmigrant alien who is currently subject to special registration as a result of the publication of any previous Federal Register notice may, while he or she remains in the United States, upon 10 days notice and at the Department of Homeland Security's discretion, be required to appear at a Department of Homeland Security Office in person to provide additional information or documentation confirming compliance with his or her visa and admission. The Department of Homeland Security will determine on a case-by-case basis, which aliens must appear in person to verify information. The nonimmigrant alien subject to special registration must appear at the designated office location, and on the specified date and time, unless otherwise specified in the notice.

Contrary to popular belief, NSEERS was not the first example of a registration requirement for foreign nationals. The INA was evoked in 1979 during the Iran Hostage Crisis requiring Iranians in the U.S. to register with the INS. Perhaps an example that more closely shadows the current NSEERS program is the Alien Registration Act of 1940 in which, during the era of McCarthyism, all resident aliens, Communists, and others considered a threat to the country were required to register with the U.S. government.[62]

Registration required a minimum of fingerprinting and photographing of the registrant, though many NSEERS participants were required to provide names and addresses of relatives, credit card and banking information, and information on any organizations to which they belonged, among other things. This data was requested under the rationale that those who were subject to NSEERS were potential terrorists and information regarding family, friends, and financing would provide insight that could help in infiltrating terrorist networks. What the U.S. government failed to recognize was that the NSEERS process was fundamentally flawed. Though the consequences for failing to register as part of NSEERS were potentially harsh, it is highly unlikely that terrorists would voluntarily go to their local INS office to register; especially since the INS did not outline a plan for finding those who did not register.

In addition to call-in registration and the registering of foreign nationals as they entered the United States, there was as a departure notification requirement in which all individuals registered in NSEERS had to complete an exit interview at their last POE before departing the United States. Failure to complete this process alone could not be basis for a consular officer to refuse the issuance of a visa to an individual. In a cable issued on May 10, 2003, several months after the NSEERS registration process began, the Department of State stated, "a visa can only be refused based on

---

62. United States. Alien Registration Act. 18 USC 2385. 29 June 1940.

reason to believe the applicant will not comply, and not on previous violation of NSEERS."[63]

The process of NSEERS, while inconvenient and perhaps overzealous on the part of the U.S. government, raises additional questions regarding civil liberties, racial profiling, and the price of security in this country. The government registered over 177,260 individuals as part of NSEERS and although they captured 143 criminals, the NSEERS report released by the Department of Homeland Security on December 1, 2003 did not account for the capture of any terrorists.[64] As Former Attorney General John Ashcroft mentioned in his remarks on November 7, 2002, "We have increased our capacity to intercept terrorists or criminals who attempt to enter the country, to verify that foreign visitors who may present national security concerns stick to their plans while they are here."[65] This may be the theory behind the implementation of NSEERS; however, there has been little evidence to indicate that much follow up was done on the government's part to see that foreign visitors registered under NSEERS "stick to their plans." Furthermore, Ashcroft goes on to say that several aliens have been arrested under NSEERS because of outstanding warrants and other immigration violations; however, in singling out citizens of certain countries we are acting as though citizens of other countries (those where we do not require mandatory NSEERS registration) are more trustworthy and honorable, which may not be justified.

The fact that the United States has targeted specific countries, rather than all countries, for the NSEERS program is troublesome at several levels. As one opponent of the program made clear, "Somebody who's completely illegal isn't going to walk into an INS office to register."[66] Moreover, the United States government has

---

63. United States. "State Department Discusses NSEERS Failure to Exit Through Departure Control." 02 STATE 186027. U.S. Department of State. Washington, 10 May 2003.

64. "Fact Sheet: Changes to National Security Entry/Exit Registration System (NSEERS)." Department of Homeland Security. Washington, 1 December 2003.

65. Ashcroft, John. "Attorney General's Remarks Implementation of NSEERS." U.S. Department of Justice. Washington, 7 November 2002.

repeatedly stated that the war on terrorism is unique in that it is not country specific. This is the reasoning that the United States government and Secretary of Defense Donald Rumsfeld give for not applying the rules of the Geneva Convention to the war on terrorism, namely that "the international rules govern wars between countries but not those involving groups such as al-Qaeda."[67] Ashcroft justified NSEERS by saying: "Aliens from other countries who warrant extra scrutiny when they visit the United States are subject to the NSEERS requirements."[68] Ashcroft fails to distinguish that by solely focusing on certain countries we may be reducing the likelihood that terrorists will be caught. Al-Qaeda has had known operatives in Germany, Spain, and Canada;[69] however, the nationals of those countries were not required to register under NSEERS.

Perhaps what is most disconcerting about NSEERS, aside from its racial profiling and potential ineffectiveness, is the perception that it creates among upstanding nonimmigrants within the United States. One NSEERS registrant explains that "I didn't even go to the police in Syria and now I have to go through these procedures...[NSEERS] makes things worse, maybe, because now I have this experience in the USA, as I told you all the security offices I have visited in my life are in the USA, which is like the 'democracy' state."[70] He, among other NSEERS registrants, stated that while the immigration officers performing the registration interview were pleasant, "the problem that I told you was this: it's like a psychological thing."[71]

---

66. Murphy, Jarrett. "Feds Detain Hundred of Immigrants." CBS News. 19 December 2002.

67. "Rummy Defends Prisoner Treatment." CBS News. ‹http://www.cbsnews.com/stories/2004/05/12/iraq/printable617105.shtml›. 12 May 2004.

68. Ashcroft, John. "Attorney General's Remarks Implementation of NSEERS." U.S. Department of Justice. Washington, 7 November 2002.

69. "Al-Qaeda in Canada?" 60 Minutes. CBS News. 1 May 2002.

70. Skeiker, Fadi. Personal interview with author. 3 August 2004.

71. *Ibid.*

Several groups within the United States spoke out against NSEERS. Senators Russell Feingold (D-WI) and Edward Kennedy (D-MA) as well as Representative John Conyers, Jr. (D-MI) drafted a letter to Attorney General John Ashcroft asserting, "We have grave doubts about whether the INS's implementation of NSEERS has struck the proper balance between securing our borders on the one hand and respecting the civil liberties of foreign students, businesspeople, and visitors who have come to our nation legally on the other."[72] NAFSA: Association of International Educators suggested that NSEERS and the detention of those who registered as part of NSEERS "should deeply trouble every American."[73]

NAFSA (formerly known as the National Association of Foreign Student Advisors) also made the point that "this situation, which is alienating both a crucial region of the world and Arab and Muslim communities in the United States, is harmful to U.S. interests and our national security, and must not be allowed to continue."[74] The American Immigration Lawyers Association[75] and the American Civil Liberties Union expressed similar concerns.

The implementation of NSEERS also incited outrage among the international community. As NSEERS affected the perception of those in the United States, it also affected the world's perception of this country. As one NSEERS registrant commented, "You are building your safety inside, but when you go outside the United States you are creating hate for you from the world."[76] Canada released a travel advisory on October 29, 2002, calling the process "discriminatory" and "unfriendly."[77] The advisory went on to say, "In

---

72. Feingold, Russell, Edward Kennedy, and John Conyers, Jr. Letter to Attorney General. 23 December 2002.

73. Oaks, Ursula. "Statement of NAFSA: Association of International Educators on Special Registration Program for Certain Nonimmigrant Visitors." NAFSA: Association of International Educators. 3 January 2003.

74. *Ibid.*

75. Golub, Judith, Charlie Miller, and Dane VandenBerg. "AILA Urges Repeal of Special Registration." American Immigration Lawyers Association. 9 January 2003.

76. Anonymous. Personal interview with author. 3 August 2004.

77. Labott, Elise. "Canada Issues U.S. Travel Warning." CNN News. ⟨http://www.cnn.com⟩. 30 October 2002.

these circumstances, the Department of Foreign Affairs and International Trade advises Canadians who were born in the above countries or who may be citizens of these countries to consider carefully whether they should attempt to enter the United States for any reason, including transit to or from third countries."[78] The Bangladeshi government mirrored the sentiments of Canada when Bangladesh was placed on the NSEERS mandatory registration list in December 2002. The Bangladeshi foreign minister made the point that "we've never seen any Bangladeshi in any terrorist attack anywhere in the world" and that Bangladesh is "fighting terrorism as our conviction, not as a convenience."[79]

As part of the NSEERS process, nearly 3,000 people were detained, though few were charged with any crimes. In his testimony David Martin, former General Counsel of the Immigration and Naturalization Service, did not voice objections to detentions *per se*; however, he did question the lengthy detentions of individuals who had not been charged with immigration violations or crimes.[80]

Since the attacks of September 11, the U.S. government has held a series of closed immigration hearings of detained individuals. The hearings pertained to those declared to be "special interest detainees" by Attorney General Ashcroft. The hearings were so secret that even other government agencies such as the INS were unable to obtain information on detainees to process their own investigations.[81] Several groups including the ACLU and the Detroit Free Press filed lawsuits citing the Freedom of Information Act, requesting the names of the individuals who had been arrested and incarcerated as part of a round up of predominantly Muslim foreign

---

78. Cohen, Tom. "Canada Issues U.S. Travel Warning." CBS News. ⟨http://www.cbsnews.com/stories/2002 /10/30/world/main527560.shtml⟩. 30 October 2002.

79. "Bangladesh 'Dismayed' at U.S. Registrations." CNN News. ⟨http://www.cnn.com⟩. 28 January 2003.

80. Testimony of David Martin, Warner-Booker Distinguished Professor of International Law, University of Virginia Law School, and former General Counsel, Immigration and Naturalization Service. Before the 9/11 Commission. 8 December 2004.

81. 9/11 Commission. *9/11 Commission Report.* Washington: GPO, 2004.

nationals in the United States after 9/11.[82] Attorney General John Ashcroft said in a statement, "For those detained by the INS, I do not think it is responsible for us, in a time of war, when our objective is to save American lives, to advertise to the opposing side that we have al-Qaeda membership in custody. When the United States is at war, I will not share valuable intelligence with our enemies."[83] The Federal Appeals Court sided with the government, allowing the Department of Justice to refuse to release information on the hearings to the public because, as the ruling avowed, "the press and public hold no First Amendment right of access. The primary national policy must be self-preservation."[84] Executive director of the ACLU, Kary Moss, responded by saying, "The implications are very serious. If none of these people have been charged with any criminal-law violations, then John Ashcroft has essentially, on his own, created two systems of justice in this country."[85]

While the immigration justice system is held in the executive branch rather than the judicial, one still must question the implications of holding individuals who have not been charged with a crime and refusing to release basic information, such as why someone is being held. It is understandable that noncitizens would not hold the same rights as citizens; however, if this is the approach taken in fighting terrorism we must recognize that it compromises the integrity of the United States government and the freedom it symbolizes. Furthermore, the deprivation of rights to one group within the United States, in the name of the war on terror, can very possibly lead to a dispossession of freedoms for American citizens as

---

82. "Federal Court to Hear Arguments May 29 in Battle Over Government Secrecy About Sept. 11 Detainees." American Civil Liberties Union. ⟨http://archive.aclu.org/features/f012302a.html⟩. 28 May 2002.

83. Ashcroft, John. Speech on Total Number of Federal Criminal Charges and INS Detainees. 27 November 2001.

84. *Center for National Security Studies v. US Department of Justice*, 215 F.Supp.2d 94 (D.D.C. 2002).

85. Audi, Tamara. "U.S. Held 600 for Secret Rulings." *Detroit Free Press*. 18 July 2002.

well. The lines between justice, freedom, and protection have been blurred significantly since 9/11.

The American-Arab Anti-Discrimination Committee, the Council on American-Islamic Relations, The Alliance of Iranian Americans, the National Council of Pakistani Americans, and six John Does brought a class action lawsuit against the Attorney General. The lawsuit is excerpted below:[86]

> Plaintiffs bring this action on behalf of themselves and all other persons similarly situated pursuant to Fed.R.Civ.Proc. Rule 23(1) and 23(b)(2). Plaintiffs provisionally propose the following class definition:
>
> All persons who are required to register with the INS pursuant to 8 U.S.C. § 1305(b) and implementing regulations and notices, and who have been or will be —
>
>> (1) arrested without warrant or probable cause to believe that they will flee before a warrant can be obtained; or
>>
>> (2) subjected to removal without any possibility of release on bond or recognizance despite being prima facie eligible to adjust their status to that of a lawful permanent resident, and who either —
>>
>>> (A) have pending applications for relief from removal pursuant to INA § 245; or
>>>
>>> (B) would become immediately eligible for relief from removal pursuant to INA § 245 were the INS to approve a pending application or petition that is predicate to eligibility for relief under INA § 245.

In addition to the detentions and closed hearings, the U.S. government asked that some 5,000 people, mostly of Middle Eastern descent, come forward for "voluntary questioning." However, it was also noted that if they were found to be in violation of their

---

86. American-Arab Anti-Discrimination Committee v. Ashcroft, 241 F.Supp.2d 1111 (C.D.Cal.2003).

immigration statuses, they would be detained.[87] Knowing that one could potentially be detained, it is highly doubtful that many would come forward to be voluntarily questioned, nor is it likely that anyone with information that the government is interested in obtaining would be willing to contact the government on this basis. Though the government stated that the people wanted for questioning were not considered terrorist suspects, it is obvious that the government was not going to question them about mundane occurrences; the government was looking for information about 9/11 and potential future attacks. This was a move that was, predictably, not very fruitful for the United States.

The actions of the U.S. government have prompted many to suggest that the attention that Muslims and Muslim-Americans are receiving is fundamentally racist. Jan Ting, Professor of Law, Temple University Beasley School of Law, and former Assistant Commissioner for Refugees, Asylum and Parole for the INS, referred to these claims as "misdirected."[88] He further stated, "The individuals subject to these initiatives are certainly being profiled, but the profiling is done on non-invidious factors such as age, gender, and the objective immigration documents presented on entry to the U.S., i.e. passports from designated countries."[89] He went on to say, "Even if these government initiatives could somehow be construed as racial or ethnic profiling, that fact would not necessarily make the practices either illegal, unconstitutional or wrong."[90] The flaw in Mr. Ting's argument is that even though something may be legal, there is nothing to say that a law may not be wrong. The United States has had a history of blatantly racist immigration laws from the Dred Scott decision to Japanese

87. "INS Memo Cites Possible Detention for Those Questioned in Terror Probe." CNN News. ‹http://www.cnn.com/2001/US/11/29/inv.terrorism.interviews/index.html›. 29 November 2001.

88. Testimony of Jan Ting, Professor of Law, Temple University Beasley School of Law, and former Assistant Commissioner for Refugees, Asylum and Parole, Immigration and Naturalization Service. Before the 9/11 Commission. 8 December 2003.

89. *Ibid.*

90. *Ibid.*

Internment; many people believe that some of the post-9/11 laws will be added to this list.

The question then becomes, how does this profiling affect immigration to the United States and the immigrants who currently reside in the country? Since 9/11 there has been a considerable increase in anti-Muslim and anti-Arab discrimination, both government-sponsored and not. In July 2004, a man by the name of Simon Abi Nader won his discrimination case against the Department of Homeland Security. In his case, he claimed he "had routinely experienced discrimination, harassment and humiliation perpetrated by high-level agency officials while employed in the Miami District Office of the Department of Homeland Security Citizenship and Immigration Services."[91] A year earlier another government official, Bassem Youseff, the highest ranking Arab-American in the FBI, filed a lawsuit claiming that he was the subject of discrimination after 9/11 because of his ethnicity and was not allowed to participate in 9/11-related investigations.[92] Five separate suits were also filed against U.S. airlines claiming racial profiling and discrimination after the terrorist attacks.[93] In the months after 9/11, nearly two hundred hate crimes against people of Middle Eastern descent were reported.[94]

While the discrimination lawsuits filed and the hate crimes that occurred shortly after September 11 are overt examples of prejudice, intolerance also took subtle forms. In a predictable move shortly after the 9/11 attacks, the INS arrested several airport employees on immigration violations.[95] The tighter enforcement of immigration laws after the 9/11 attacks forced many undocumented

---

91. "Arab American Wins Jury Verdict of $305,000 in Employment Discrimination Case vs. Department of Homeland Security and Department of Justice." Arab-American Anti-Discrimination Committee. ‹http://www.adc.org/index.php?id=2293›. 30 July 2004.

92. "Agent Sues FBI for Discrimination." CNN News. ‹http://www.cnn.com/2003/LAW/07/ 20/fbi.bias.suit/index.html›. 20 July 2003.

93. "Airlines Face Post 9/11 Racial Profiling/Discrimination Suits." CNN News. ‹http://archives.cnn.com/2002/LAW/06/04/airlines.discrimination/index.html›. 4 June 2002.

94. "Ashcroft, Muslim Leaders to Discuss Hate Crimes." CNN News. ‹http://archives.cnn.com/2001/US/10/16/rec.justice.antimuslim/index.html›. 16 October 2004.

aliens in the United States to flee the country, often heading to Canada seeking asylum. Though it is understandable that tighter immigration enforcement would be implemented after the terrorist attack, there was a pattern as to who was targeted. There are significant numbers of illegal immigrants throughout the United States, yet only a small portion felt the change in policy. It is unrealistic to think that people from a certain area of the world are the only ones who pose a threat, and not only that but also to think that only illegal immigrants are threatening. It is quite possible that individuals who are completely legal in immigration status can be a danger to the United States, as some of the 9/11 hijackers were.

It is suspected that the number of visas that have been denied to those from countries deemed to be affiliated with terrorist organizations has increased, though this information is not public and is exempt from the Freedom of Information Act. In an interview, the press officer for the Bureau of Consular Affairs in the Department of State insisted that there had been no changes in the number of denials, but rather that fewer people had applied for visas immediately after 9/11. She did state that applications for visas had increased in recent months, but refused to disclose information regarding visa denial rates for certain countries or how denial rates compare among countries.[96]

Visa issuance procedures have changed since 9/11. It is now required that visa applicants (with some exceptions) have a personal interview with a consular officer. During the interview the officer will be looking for grounds for inadmissibility into the U.S. such as any health concerns, a criminal history, terrorist affiliations, whether the applicant would become a public charge to the U.S., whether the applicant would be likely to try to obtain unauthorized employment in the country, any past immigration violations including removal from the U.S., and, if the applicant is a

---

95. "INS Arrests Washington-Area Airport Employees." CNN News. ‹http://archives.cnn.com/2002/TRAVEL/NEWS/04/23/ins.airport.arrests/index.html›. 23 April 2003.

96. Shannon, Kelly. Personal interview with author. 24 June 2004.

nonimmigrant, proof that the applicant will return to the home country, among other things.[97]

Visa application procedures changed under the Enhanced Border Security and Visa Entry Reform Act. Signed into law by President Bush on May 14, 2002, the law changed and enhanced many procedures regarding visa issuance and entry into the United States. Consulates and embassies were now required to create a terrorist lookout committee to locate known and suspected terrorists within their jurisdiction, to share that information with other agencies within the U.S., and to input the names of those terrorists into the appropriate databases.[98] In regards to sharing information, the law specifically mentions that the Department of State must share with what was then the INS the data file information of all those who were issued visas. Given the fact that this section was included in the Enhanced Border Security Act, one can assume that this information sharing was not in place, or was not done with regularity prior to being mandated by law. It is problematic to think that prior to this law valuable information was not being exchanged between the department that issues visas and the agency that reviews those visas to determine eligibility to enter the United States.

It seems obvious that an exchange of information of this sort would be a common procedure in U.S. immigration practices because such efforts can help to prevent visa fraud and can prevent those who should not be entering the U.S. from doing so. While the Enhanced Border Security Act mandated procedures such as this information sharing, the February 2004 report by the Congressional Research Service of the Library of Congress noted that, "whether these provisions are being successful implemented remains an important policy question."[99]

---

97. U.S. Congressional Research Service, Library of Congress. *Visa Issuances: Policy, Issues, and Legislation.* Washington: GPO. 11 February 2004.

98. P.L. 107-173. Enhanced Border Security and Visa Entry Reform Act of 2002. 14 May 2002.

Another aspect of the Enhanced Border Security and Visa Entry Reform Act that raises concerns about the integrity of the visa application process prior to the enactment of this law is that §305 outlines training that consular officers should be given regarding screening applicants for potential terrorist connections. The section in part states:

> The Secretary of State shall require that all consular officers responsible for adjudicating visa applications, before undertaking to perform consular responsibilities, receive specialized training in the effective screening of visa applicants who pose a potential threat to the safety or security of the United States.[100]

If anything, the need to include such a provision in the law suggests that prior to 9/11 security was not at the forefront of the agenda for consular officers. Given the fact that U.S. entities throughout the 1990s, including two U.S. embassies, were targets of terrorist attacks, one would have thought that "specialized training" on how to recognize those who may be a threat to the U.S. would have been thoroughly implemented long before this Act.

The problem may be a structural weakness within the State Department; visa issuance work is a low level job for foreign service officers. As explained in the *Foreign Service Journal*, "The CA [Consular Affairs] officers — often the junior-most Foreign Service employees — have to play both the role of welcoming envoy to the millions of visitors who want to come to the United States each year to have fun, to do business, or to study, and the role of stern security guard against terrorists and criminals who would do America harm."[101] But, as Martin Tatuch explained at a NAFSA: Association of International Educators regional conference in November 2004, "[9/11 brought] a different attitude of how we do consular work."[102]

---

99. U.S. Congressional Research Service, Library of Congress. *Visa Issuances: Policy, Issues, and Legislation.* Washington, D.C.: GPO. 11 February 2004.

100. P.L. 107-173.

101. Zeller, Shawn. "The Brave New World of Visa Processing." *Foreign Service Journal.* September 2004.

A process called "Visa Mantis" was in place long before the Enhanced Border Security Act. Visa Mantis was first implemented in the visa application process during the Cold War. Guidance for Visa Mantis comes under INA §212(a)(3)(A)(i)(ii), which deals primarily with the unauthorized transfer of technology and potential violations of U.S. export laws. Under Visa Mantis, the applicant's name is submitted for a security review. Only when the security review is completed can a decision regarding the issuance of a visa be made. The process mostly affects students and scholars coming to the United States to study or to conduct research.

There are also the Visa Condor, the Visa Donkey, and the Visa Eagle (it's a real zoo over there at the Department of State!). Visa Condor is responsible for many of the delays in the visa issuance process. Rather than a security clearance in which the applicant's information is sent to Washington for a full security review, Visa Condor is a thirty-day delay period in the issuing of a visa. The thirty days give cooperating agencies time to voice objections to the visa issuance. If no agency provides information that would exclude the issuance of a visa, then the applicant will be given one after the thirty-day waiting period.[103] Visa Eagle requires a ten-day waiting period and is used for applicants who are being sponsored by the U.S. Government to come to the United States. Visa Donkey, a more complex procedure, requires authorization from the Department of State before a visa may be issued to an applicant and is used for those who would not qualify for the Visa Eagle procedures.[104]

Those most affected by Visa Mantis are international students and scholars trying to come to the United States for academic or research reasons. The Technology Alert List, created during the

---

102. Tatuch, Martin. "The Consular Officer: Facilitator or Obstructer in International Education?" at NAFSA Region XI Conference. 18 November 2004.

103. Testimony of Janice Jacobs, Deputy Assistant Secretary for Visa Services U.S. Department of State. Before the Committee on Science, U.S. House of Representatives. 26 March 2003.

104. "Visa Mantis Program Modified." NAFSA: Association of International Educators. ‹http://www.nafsa.org/content/ProfessionalandEducationalResources/Immigration AdvisingResources/b9.htm›. 24 August 1999.

Cold War, covers sixteen majors/areas of study that require automatic security checks before a visa can be issued.[105] After 9/11, the list was divided into two parts: Part A, the "Critical Fields List," and Part B, a list of countries that the U.S. government deems to need additional attention for "political, security, or foreign policy reasons."[106]

Technology Alert List

Advanced ceramics: Technologies related to the production of tanks, military vehicles, and weapons systems.

Advanced computer/microelectronic technology: Technologies associated with superconductivity supercomputing, microcomputer compensated crystal oscillators.

Aircraft and missile propulsion and vehicular systems: Technologies associated with liquid and solid-rocket propulsion systems, missile propulsion, rocket staging/separation mechanisms, aerospace thermal and high-performance structures.

Chemical and biotechnology engineering: Technologies associated with the development or production of biological and toxin agents, pathogenics, biological weapons research.

Conventional munitions: Technologies associated with warhead and large caliber projectiles, fusing and arming systems.

High-performance metals and alloys: Technologies associated with military applications.

Information security: Technologies associated with cryptographic systems to ensure secrecy of communications.

Lasers and directed energy systems: Technologies associated with laser-guided bombs, ranging devices, countering missiles.

Marine technology: Technology associated with submarines and deep submersible vessels, marine propulsion systems designed for

---

105. 9 FAM 40.31 Exhibit I Page 2 of 3 9 FAM 40.31 Exhibit I Page 3 of 3. "Technology Alert List." 22 May 2000.
106. 9 FAM 501. "General Guidance." 24 April 2002.

undersea use and navigation, radar, acoustic/nonacoustic detection.

Materials technology: Technologies related to the production of composite materials for structural functions in aircraft, spacecraft, undersea vehicles and missiles.

Missile/missile technology: Technologies associated with air vehicles and unmanned missile systems.

Navigation and guidance control: Technologies associated with the delivery and accuracy of unguided and guided weapons, such as tracking and homing devices, internal navigation systems, vehicle and flight control systems.

Nuclear technology: Technologies associated with the production and use of nuclear material for military applications.

Remote imaging and reconnaissance: Technologies associated with military reconnaissance efforts, such as drones, remotely piloted or unmanned vehicles, imagery systems, high-resolution cameras.

Robotics: Technologies associated with artificial intelligence, computer-controlled machine tools.

Sensors: Technology associated with marine acoustics, missile launch calibration, night vision devices, high-speed photographic equipment.

The Technology Alert List is no longer a public document;[107] however, the most recent public version of the list included several areas of focus that would require a review by the government before a visa would be issued.

In May 2004, a bill intended to improve the Visa Mantis system was introduced before the House of Representatives. With 20,000 Visa Mantis security checks performed during 2003, it can be expected that delays would ensue. The bill introduced by Rep. Michael Capuano (D-MA) would allow the results of a Visa Mantis clearance to be valid for three years, would allow for revalidation to

107. Tatuch, Martin. "The Consular Officer: Facilitator or Obstructer in International Education?" at NAFSA Region XI Conference. 18 November 2004.

occur within the U.S., and would allow portability of clearance in changes of status; it would improve the training that consular officers receive in regards to Visa Mantis, and mandates that the Secretary of State improve the specificity of the Technology Alert List.[108] As of February 2005, the State Department did ease the annual application requirement by extending the validity of science-related visas to up to four years.

Foreign students and visiting scholars are a group that has not had much support post 9/11. Though security clearances are an important component to the visa application process, delays while waiting for those clearances can have a detrimental effect on applicants. Furthermore, after the attacks of 9/11, speaking out against increased security measures in immigration laws was largely viewed as un-American and unpatriotic. As an official at one prominent university explained in regard to the Visa Mantis delays that often extended for months, "professors start and they say, 'I want to write letters, I'm going to call my congressman,' but we've been told by the State Department to stay out of it."[109] A 2004 GAO report, entitled "Improvements Needed to Reduce Time Taken to Adjudicate Visas for Science Students and Scholars," found that the Visa Mantis process often took excessive amounts of time to complete, sometimes taking longer than 120 days. This can be highly inconvenient for students and scholars who have specific start dates and deadlines that must be met. In response to the GAO report, the Department of State issued a statement that countered, "The report does not recognize the key role that the Visa Mantis screening process plays in protecting U.S. national security, particularly in combating the proliferation of weapons of mass destruction, their delivery systems, and conventional weapons."[110]

---

108. American Council on Education. "Bill Addressing Visa Mantis System Introduced in House." ‹http://www.acenet.edu/hena/readArticle.cfm?articleID=748›. 19 May 2004.

109. Anonymous. Personal interview with author. 2 June 2004.

110. "Improvements Needed to Reduce Time Taken to Adjudicate Visas for Science Students and Scholars." GAO-04-371. General Accounting Office. Washington: GPO, February 2004.

Indeed, this point has been the topic of much discussion in recent years with Rahid Taha al-Azawi al-Tikriti, a.k.a. Iraq's "Dr. Germ," having received a doctorate from the U.K.'s University of East Anglia in plant biology where she researched botulism and anthrax and is believed to have ordered biological samples from the U.S.[111] The FBI and the Former Attorney General Ashcroft have also listed a former MIT student and Pakistani national, Aafia Siddiqui, as a terrorist suspect. Siddiqui completed her doctoral studies at MIT in neurological sciences.[112] Suspicions that future Aafia Siddiquis and "Dr. Germs" will try to study in the U.S. has made the Visa Mantis system a common routine in some visa issuances.

The Enhanced Border Security and Visa Entry Reform Act also outlined the development and implementation of an entry/exit system. One way in which the United States can more effectively and fairly monitor nonimmigrants who are in the country is to create systems and policies that apply to all, not to specific groups. Indeed, part of the reasoning for eliminating NSEERS (aside from the fact that no, or very few, terrorists were caught as part of the program) was the fact that the implementation of the United States Visitor and Immigrant Status Indicator Technology (US-VISIT). US-VISIT requires that non-immigrant visa applicants be fingerprinted and photographed during the application process and during entry into the United States. Such steps are being taken to reduce instances of visa fraud and to aid in the review of watchlists and databases.[113]

The Department of Homeland Security has outlined four goals for the US-VISIT program: to "enhance the security of U.S. citizens and visitors, facilitate legitimate travel and trade, ensure the integrity of the immigration system, and safeguard the personal privacy of visitors."[114] It is not completely clear how collecting

---

111. "Iraq's Dr. Germ Detained." BBC News. ‹http://news.bbc.co.uk/2/hi/middle_east/3021481.stm›. 12 May 2003.

112. "FBI Shows Images of Suspects in Terror Warning." *The Boston Globe.* ‹http://www.thebostonchannel.com/print/3346122/detail.html?use=print›. 26 May 2004.

113. "Fact Sheet: U.S. Land Borders." Department of Homeland Security.

biometric information on individuals "safeguards the personal privacy of visitors,"[115] though the goal of assisting lawful travel into the U.S. is a commendable aspiration. It remains questionable, however, how US-VISIT, as it is utilized presently, will achieve the other intended goals. Collecting biometric information during the visa application process and reviewing the information when that individual enters the United States is a worthy effort that will aid in the detection of some instances of visa fraud; however, no system is error proof. Furthermore, this is only one small aspect of the program that will aid in the enhancement of the security of the country. The biometric information may be collected and compared against national databases; however, unless a name is in the database, US-VISIT will have no additional benefits in preventing terrorism. Tim Edgar, legislative counsel for the ACLU, made this point when he stated, "The problem with 9/11 is that we didn't know who the terrorists were. We could have put them through this system and they would have gotten through without any problem."[116]

In addition to the security flaws the US-VISIT system poses, it is uncertain how the system will "ensure the integrity of the immigration system." The system is a good one in theory; however, without proper use and monitoring of the system, US-VISIT, like other immigration systems in place such as NSEERS or SEVIS, it will be completely useless. It should be noted that while US-VISIT began in January 2004, it wasn't until September 2004 that those entering the U.S. under the VWP were required to register with US-VISIT. Furthermore, VWP participants were included in US-VISIT only after a report from the DHS's Office of Inspector General criticizing of omission of those entering the U.S. through the VWP. To truly make security a priority would require the inclusion of all nonimmigrants in a system such as US-VISIT.

---

114. "US-VISIT." Department of Homeland Security. 2004.

115. "US-VISIT Fact Sheet." Department of Homeland Security. 2003.

116. "U.S. Ready to Fingerprint Visitors." CNN News. <http://www.cnn.com/2004/US/01/04/fingerprint.program/index.html>. 5 January 2004.

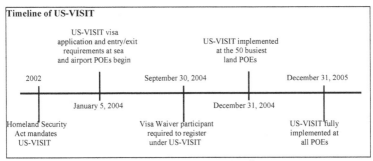

The system raises more questions than it answers. For instance, the current system allows for the exemption of certain visa holders from participating in US-VISIT, namely diplomatic and NATO visa holders.[117] Though the system is being utilized to reduce visa fraud, US-VISIT could have far-reaching immigration possibilities. With US-VISIT, immigration officials would be able to tell when an individual overstayed a visa. The program could be expanded to include the U.S. address during the stay of the nonimmigrant, which would be valuable if someone is suspected of terrorist or criminal activity. It would also eliminate the need for SEVIS, and would monitor all noncitizens within the country more equally, rather than targeting specific groups while virtually ignoring others. Presently, it is unclear how US-VISIT will be monitored apart from the initial review of information during entry into the U.S. Without the consistent monitoring and utilization of the system for all visa holders entering the country, the system will not provide additional security for the United States, nor will it guarantee the veracity of the current immigration system data within this country.

The implementation of US-VISIT comes just as the United States is beginning to recover from the decline in nonimmigrant visits after 9/11. In 2002, nonimmigrants coming to the U.S., of which 87% were tourists or business travelers, declined by 15% from

---

117. Federal Register. "Implementation of the United States Visitor and Immigrant Status Indicator Technology Program ("US-VISIT"); Biometric Requirements." 5 January 2004.

the previous year (about 28 million total in 2002, according to the Migration Policy Institute). Of those coming to the U.S., less than one percent came from Asian Islamic countries, and the majority came from just ten countries (U.K., Mexico, Japan, Germany, France, South Korea, China, Italy, Brazil, and the Netherlands).[118] Foreign tourism has a tremendous effect on the U.S. economy. In 2000, approximately 50.9 million foreign travelers came to the United States.[119] Given this number of people, the economic impact that foreign tourism has on the United States is vast and a slowdown in the U.S. tourism industry can have serious repercussions. Already hurt by the decline in visitors to the U.S. after 9/11, the tourism industry fears that newly implemented stricter immigration policies will contribute to the reduction in numbers of foreign nationals traveling to the country.

Tourism in the U.S. is an immense and powerful industry and it actively lobbies government officials for measures that would aid in the growth of the industry. Though it is important to recognize the fundamental role foreign tourists play within the economy, it remains a challenge to balance that benefit against the need to tighten immigration regulations. The majority of the 9/11 hijackers and the terrorists during the 1993 WTC bombing were in the United States as tourists. It remains a difficult task to create immigration laws that allow for *bona fide* tourists who pose no security threat to obtain visas and enter the U.S. with minimal inconveniences, yet have policies that work to protect the country against future attacks.

It cannot be expected that the structural, managerial, and political challenges that face the agencies that control immigration in the United States will be overcome quickly. As the call for reform to strengthen immigration policies in an effort to protect the country against future terrorist attacks rings clear, it is important to

---

118. Coffey, Colleen. *Coming to America Two Years After 9/11.* Washington: Migration Policy Institute, 2003.

119. "International Visitors Boost U.S. Economy." U.S. International Trade Administration. ‹http://tinet.ita.doc.gov/tinews/archive/20010425.html›. 25 April 2001.

develop laws that work to both welcome those who have justly entered the U.S. and to keep out those who intend to harm the country and its people. To develop policies that do not address the immigrant population as a whole is to underestimate the intelligence of terrorists. Policies with limited scope, such as NSEERS, create loopholes in the immigration system that invite exploitation. Creation of fair and effective policies requires the commitment, support, and combined efforts of agencies throughout the U.S. government. n the absence of this cooperation, the agencies that control immigration will be set up for failure and ultimately will open the doors for future attacks.

In an editorial for the *Washington Post*, former Secretary of Homeland Security Tom Ridge said, "we have built higher barriers to terrorism and better bridges to each other."[120] And yet, it appears that there has been more emphasis on barriers and considerably less on bridges. Immigration plays an integral role in the United States and it is in the best interest of the country and its citizens as a whole to embrace comprehensive immigration laws as a way to deter terrorism by fostering positive relations with immigrants while working to dissuade terrorists from entering.

---

120. Ridge, Tom. "Since That Day..." *Washington Post.* 11 September 2003. A23.

4. SEVIS AND INTERNATIONAL STUDENTS

Hani Hanjour, Ahmed Alghamdi, Mohammed Atta, and Marwan Al-Shehhi all received student visas.[1] Although this sad fact may have given the impetus to get a national database of foreign students fully functional in the year 2003, they were not the impetus for the creation of such a database.

The initial regulations calling for the creation of a national database of foreign students came from §641 of the Illegal Immigration Reform and Immigrant Responsibility Act (IIRIRA) of 1996. In §641,[2] the act states:

> SEC. 641. Program to Collect Information Relating to Nonimmigrant Foreign Students and Other Exchange Program Participants.
>
> In General. —
>
> (1) Program. — The Attorney General, in consultation with the Secretary of State and the Secretary of Education, shall develop and conduct a program to collect from approved institutions of higher education and

---

1. "INS Releases Legal Status of Alleged Hijackers." CNN News. ‹http://archives.cnn.com/2001/US/10/11/inv.ins.hijackers/index.html›. 11 October 2001.

2. P.L. 104-208. Illegal Immigration Reform and Immigrant Responsibility Act. §303(e). 30 September 1996.

designated exchange visitor programs in the United States the information described in subsection (c) with respect to aliens who—

(A) have the status, or are applying for the status, of nonimmigrants under subparagraph (F), (J), or (M) of section 101(a)(15) of the Immigration and Nationality Act; and

(B) are nationals of the countries designated under subsection (b).

(2) Deadline. — The program shall commence not later than January 1, 1998.

(b) Covered Countries. — The Attorney General, in consultation with the Secretary of State, shall designate countries for purposes of subsection (a)(1)(B). The Attorney General shall initially designate not less than 5 countries and may designate additional countries at any time while the program is being conducted.

(c) Information to be Collected. —

(1) In general. — The information for collection under subsection (a) with respect to an alien consists of —

(A) the identity and current address in the United States of the alien;

(B) the nonimmigrant classification of the alien and the date on which a visa under the classification was issued or extended or the date on which a change to such classification was approved by the Attorney General;

(C) in the case of a student at an approved institution of higher education, the current academic status of the alien, including whether the alien is maintaining status as a full-time student or, in the case of a participant in a designated exchange visitor program, whether the alien is satisfying the terms and conditions of such program; and

(D) in the case of a student at an approved institution of higher education, any disciplinary action taken by the institution against the alien as a result of the alien's being convicted of a crime or, in the case of a participant in a designated exchange visitor program, any change in the alien's participation as a result of the alien's being convicted of a crime.

(2) FERPA. — The Family Educational Rights and Privacy Act of 1974 shall not apply to aliens described in subsection (a) to the extent that the Attorney General determines necessary to carry out the program under subsection (a).

(3) Electronic collection. — The information described in paragraph (1) shall be collected electronically, where practicable.

(4) Computer software.—

(A) Collecting institutions. — To the extent practicable, the Attorney General shall design the program in a manner that permits approved institutions of higher education and designated exchange visitor programs to use existing software for the collection, storage, and data processing of information described in paragraph (1).

(B) Attorney general. — To the extent practicable, the Attorney General shall use or enhance existing software for the collection, storage, and data processing of information described in paragraph (1).

(d) Participation by Institutions of Higher Education and Exchange Visitor Programs.—

(1) Condition. — The information described in subsection (c) shall be provided by as a condition of—

(A) in the case of an approved institution of higher education, the continued approval of the institution under subparagraph (F) or (M) of section 101(a)(15) of the Immigration and Nationality Act; and in the case of an approved institution of higher education or a designated exchange visitor program, the granting of authority to issue documents to an alien demonstrating the alien's eligibility for a visa under subparagraph (F), (J), or (M) of section 101(a)(15) of such Act.

(2) Effect of failure to provide information. — If an approved institution of higher education or a designated exchange visitor program fails to provide the specified

information, such approvals and such issuance of visas shall be revoked or denied.

(e) Funding.—

(1) In general. — Beginning on April 1, 1997, an approved institution of higher education and a designated exchange visitor program shall impose on, and collect from, each alien described in paragraph (3), with respect to whom the institution or program is required by subsection (a) to collect information, a fee established by the Attorney General under paragraph (4) at the time—

(A) when the alien first registers with the institution or program after entering the United States; or

(B) in a case where a registration under subparagraph (A) does not exist, when the alien first commences activities in the United States with the institution or program.

(2) visitor program shall remit the fees collected under paragraph (1) to the Attorney General pursuant to a schedule established by the Attorney General.

(3) Aliens described. — An alien referred to in paragraph (1) is an alien who has nonimmigrant status under subparagraph (F), (J), or (M) of section 101(a)(15) of the Immigration and Nationality Act (other than a nonimmigrant under section 101(a)(15)(J) of such Act who has come to the United States as a participant in a program sponsored by the Federal Government).

(4) Amount and use of fees.—

(A) Establishment of amount. — The Attorney General shall establish the amount of the fee to be imposed on, and collected from, an alien under paragraph (1). Except as provided in subsection (g)(2), the fee imposed on any individual may not exceed $100. The amount of the fee shall be based on the Attorney General's estimate of the cost per alien of conducting the information collection program described in this section.

(B) Use. — Fees collected under paragraph (1) shall be deposited as offsetting receipts into the Immigration

Examinations Fee Account (established under section 286(m) of the Immigration and Nationality Act) and shall remain available until expended for the Attorney General to reimburse any appropriation the amount paid out of which is for expenses in carrying out this section.

(f) Joint Report. — Not later than 4 years after the commencement of the program established under subsection (a), the Attorney General, the Secretary of State, and the Secretary of Education shall jointly submit to the Committees on the Judiciary of the Senate and the House of Representatives a report on the operations of the program and the feasibility of expanding the program to cover the nationals of all countries.

(g) Worldwide Applicability of the Program.—

(1) Expansion of program.—

(A) In general. — Not later than 6 months after the submission of the report required by subsection (f), the Attorney General, in consultation with the Secretary of State and the Secretary of Education, shall commence expansion of the program to cover the nationals of all countries.

(B) Deadline. — Such expansion shall be completed not later than 1 year after the date of the submission of the report referred to in subsection (f).

(2) Revision of fee. — After the program has been expanded, as provided in paragraph (1), the Attorney General may, on a periodic basis, revise the amount of the fee imposed and collected under subsection (e) in order to take into account changes in the cost of carrying out the program.

(h)Definitions. — As used in this section:

(1) Approved institution of higher education. — The term "approved institution of higher education" means a college or university approved by the Attorney General, in consultation with the Secretary of Education, under

subparagraph (F), (J), or (M) of section 101(a)(15) of the Immigration and Nationality Act.

(2) Designated exchange visitor program. — The term "designated exchange visitor program" means a program that has been—

(A) designated by the Director of the United States Information Agency for

purposes of section 101(a)(15)(J) of the Immigration and Nationality Act; and

(B) selected by the Attorney General for purposes of the program under this section.

With an implementation date of January 1, 1998, the government was set the task of creating a system that tracked individuals on F (students), M (vocational training), and J (exchange visitors) nonimmigrant visas. As a first step towards this goal, the Coordinated Interagency Partnership Regulating International Students (CIPRIS) was created as a preliminary interagency system used to monitor individuals entering on these visa types. The system, a first of its kind, would be Internet based and would serve as a liaison between students, schools, and the government. Under CIPRIS, schools and sponsors would be responsible for reporting to the INS any "events" or changes to a student's program. As explained in the December 21, 1999 Federal Register, "These notifications, made electronically through the system, will immediately inform the [Immigration and Naturalization] Service of changes in student or exchange visitor status."[3]

CIPRIS was largely met with opposition. NAFSA: Association of International Educators, an organization dedicated to promoting international education exchange, strongly opposed the implementation of CIPRIS, and backed CIPRIS-repeal legislation

---

3. Federal Register. "Illegal Immigration Reform and Immigrant Responsibility Act of 1996; Nonimmigrant Foreign Students and Other Exchange Program Participants-F, J, and M Classifications; Fee Collection Authorization." 21 December 1999.

sponsored by Senator Judd Gregg (R-NH), urging members to write their senators in support of such a bill. Opposition to CIPRIS largely centered on the proposed fee collection methods as designated in §641(e) of IIRIRA, the system's "excessive reliance on technology,"[4] and the implementation timeline. Others within the international education community feared that such a system would force school officials to "become INS representatives or investigators."[5]

While CIPRIS was implemented as a requirement of IIRIRA, it was only a pilot program and was not designed to extend beyond the trial period. In a memo from the Department of Justice's Office of Programs, Michael Cronin stated that "based on lessons learned from the CIPRIS pilot, customer and stakeholder feedback, the needs of INS's partner federal agencies, the requirements outlined in §641 of IIRIRA, and the INS mission and goals, system design work began on a new electronic system."[6] This memorandum, released in July 2001, continues with discussion of what the replacing system, SEVIS, will encompass.

STUDENT MONITORING PROGRAM ACRONYMS

CIPRIS — Coordinated Interagency Partnership Regulating International Students; the pilot for SEVP

SEVP — Student and Exchange Visitor Program; the government initiative to monitor foreign students through a variety of means including a national database to track students

---

4. "Issue Brief: Halt Implementation of SEVP/CIPRIS." NAFSA: Association of International Educators. ‹http://www.nafsa.org/content/PublicPolicy/NAFSAontheissues/CIPRIS_issue_brief_-_halt_implementation.htm›. 18 September 2000.

5. Snell, Theron P. NAFSA Listserve. October 2, 2000.

6. Cronin, Michael. "Name Change to the Coordinated Interagency Partnership Regulating International Students (CIPRIS) Memorandum." U.S. Department of Justice. Washington, 20 July 2001.

ISEAS — Interim Student and Exchange Authentication System; operated by the Department of State, a database used to track foreign students before SEVIS was implemented

SEVIS — Student and Exchange Visitor Information System; a national database with information on foreign students studying in the United States

Part of the push to incorporate $641 into IIRIRA came from the fact that Eyad Ismoil, one of the convicted conspirators of the 1993 World Trade Center (WTC) bombing, entered the United States in 1989 on a student visa for Wichita State University.[7] Since the WTC bombing, much focus has been placed on the international student as America's primary threat. International students and scholars as a population were already monitored more closely than other international populations within the United States prior to the WTC bombing. Student and exchange visitors can continue to be monitored closely with the assistance of school officials and sponsoring agencies.

Though the attack of 1993 may have been the inspiration for creating the policies of $641, even with the CIPRIS system in place, accurately tracking international students was not a forte of the INS. As the Justice Department's Office of Inspector General pointed out in a report issued after 9/11, "The INS's foreign student program has been dysfunctional, and the INS has acknowledged for several years that it does not know how many foreign students are in the United States."[8]

Also mentioned in the memorandum by Michael Cronin was the name change of CIPRIS to the Student and Exchange Visitor Program (SEVP). This program, like CIPRIS, works with schools that admit international students to track and monitor them through a series of checking mechanisms including the use of a national database that manages the data of all foreign students

---

7. "Last World Trade Center Bombing Conspirator Sentenced." CNN News. ‹http://cnn.com/US/9804/03/wtc/bombing›. 3 April 1998.

8. United States. Office of Inspector General. "The Immigration and Naturalization Service's Contacts With Two September 11 Terrorists." 20 May 2002: 12.

studying in the United States.[9] SEVP is the umbrella term for all the components that encompass the requirements as stated in §641 of IIRIRA.

The academic community initially met SEVP with great resistance. NAFSA referred to the proposed tracking system as "cumbersome and ill-conceived,"[10] while the American Association of Collegiate Registrars and Admissions Officers (AACRAO), although supportive of the system, also expressed concerns about it, particularly the new role of school officials and the proposed fee for the new system.[11]

Of course, with the events of September 11, thoughts and feelings on SEVP changed drastically. While many within the international education community originally saw SEVP as a system based on an unfounded threat, 9/11 changed that perception. Nine days after the terrorist attacks, NAFSA, one of the most vocal opponents of SEVP, released a statement saying, "We no longer oppose the foreign student tracking system that is being implemented by the INS. The time for debate on this matter is over, and the time to devise a considered response to terrorism has arrived."[12]

Student visas were issued to Hani Hanjour, Ahmed Alghamdi, Mohammed Atta, and Marwan Al-Shehhi.[13] Hani Hanjour entered the United States on a student visa from an ELS Language Center in California, Ahmed Alghamdi on one from the Defense Language Institute at Lackland Air Force Base in San Antonio, Texas, and Mohammed Atta and Marwan Al-Shehhi changed their status from

---

9. United States. "Student and Exchange Visitor Program." U.S. Immigration and Naturalization Service. Washington, 20 December 2002.

10. "Issue Brief: Halt Implementation of SEVP/CIPRIS." NAFSA: Association of International Educators. ‹http://www.nafsa.org/content/PublicPolicy/NAFSAontheissues/ CIPRIS_issue_brief_-_halt_implementation.htm›. 18 September 2000.

11. "AACRAO Comments to INS on CIPRIS Proposed Rule." AACRAO. 22 February 2000.

12. Johnson, Marlene. NAFSA Statement Before the National Press Club Policy Forum. 14 July 2003.

13. "INS Releases Legal Status of Alleged Hijackers." CNN News. ‹http:// archives.cnn.com/2001/US/ 10/11/inv.ins.hijackers/index.html›. 11 October 2001.

tourist visa to student visa so they could attend a flight training school. Hanjour, like many of the other terrorists involved in the attacks on 9/11, was out of status during the time of the attacks.

Students became the target of scrutiny for two reasons. In addition to the fact that some of the perpetrators in both the September 11 attacks and the bombing of the WTC in 1993 were listed as students, it is far more feasible to track students than many other visa types. Schools and sponsoring agencies had already been required to keep some tabs on students. Also, given the fact that schools and sponsoring agencies such as the Fulbright Foundation, Amideast, and EF were required to issue documents to each student (an I-20 for F and M visas, or a DS-2019 for J visas), in order for the student or exchange visitor to obtain a visa, it was considerably easier to follow the foreign student population more closely. Much of the tracking responsibilities could be delegated to the schools that would be admitting these individuals and issuing immigration-related documents to them.

Launched on September 11, 2002, the first actual computer database monitoring foreign students and those applying for student visas, a component within SEVP, was called the Interim Student and Exchange Authentication System (ISEAS). It was designated under the Enhanced Border Security and Visa Entry Reform Act and implemented through the U.S. Department of State. With ISEAS, every school that issued a Form I-20 (the authorization form used to obtain F visas) or DS-2019 (for J visas), must be reported to the ISEAS database. In theory, this data would be accessible to all U.S. consulates and embassies abroad within twenty-four hours of the data being entered into the system; thus, they could verify a student's acceptance to a school in the United States and the issuance of a Form I-20 or DS-2019 by the school.[14]

---

14. Bell, Larry. ‹larry.bell@colorado.edu› "Update: The Interim Student and Exchange Authentication System." Sevislist via NAFSA Listserve. 30 September 2002.

IMMIGRATION FORMS FOR STUDENTS AND EXCHANGE VISITORS

Form I-17 — Two-part form that allocates a PDSO and DSOs and serves as signature confirmation; this form is used to apply for SEVIS certification and the ability for a school to issue I-20s and/or DS-2019s

Form I-20 — Form issued to international students and used to obtain and maintain F or M nonimmigrant visa status; Form I-20AB is issued for F visas, and Form I-20MN is issued for M visas

DS-2019 — Form issued to international exchange visitors and used to obtain and maintain nonimmigrant visa status; this form is administered by the Department of State

Unfortunately, there was some lagtime between the implementation of the system and its actual use by consulates and embassies. Some consulates and embassies, such as the U.S. embassy in São Paulo, Brazil often asked that acceptance be verified through email from the school and would not issue a visa to the student until the email was received. Furthermore, with the use of SEVIS in the beginning of 2003, ISEAS was phased out, much to the surprise of some embassies and consulates. Confusion among consulates, embassies, and the international education community ensued following the demise of ISEAS.

By the time ISEAS was put into operation by the Department of State, several schools had begun using the SEVIS database, a database monitored by the INS, under the Department of Justice. Schools used SEVIS to track their international students, and because of a lack of information sharing between the governmental agencies, schools were required to report much of the same information twice. Terry Hartle, Senior Vice President of the American Council on Education, raised this concern during a subcommittee hearing on September 18, 2002. Hartle stated, "Known as the Interim Student and Exchange Authentication System (ISEAS), this is, in essence, a pre-SEVIS electronic tracking system with somewhat different requirements than we expect to face under SEVIS."[15] It is a matter of conjecture why ISEAS was implemented when SEVIS was just months away from being fully instated. One can speculate that perhaps the government did not think that SEVIS would be fully operational by the January 1, 2003 date as required under the USA PATRIOT Act. However, this also raises questions as to why it was the Department of State that created and implemented a preliminary system such as ISEAS, rather than the INS, and why there was little communication or information sharing between the two systems, much to the discontent of the schools and sponsoring agencies required to use these systems.

It was IRIIRA that first created the law mandating a system to track international students, but it was the USA PATRIOT Act that made the system a priority. In the terrorist attack of 2001, which served as a great push to invigorate the moribund project to implement a national database for tracking foreign students, only four of the nineteen highjackers were students.[16] And while it was the first World Trade Center bombing in 1993 that was the push for the incorporation of §641 into IRIIRA, only one of the six individuals convicted in the bombing was a student. It is questionable why so much emphasis was placed specifically on students, when the majority of these terrorists entered the country not as students, but rather as tourists. Monitoring students studying in the United States and maintaining accurate records of where they live, their academic status, and any criminal convictions they may have, among others things, is a positive step toward protecting this country. However, monitoring one group while virtually ignoring others is no way to ensure safety. As one student commented, "Someone who's a terrorist can get in here with other types of visas."[17] The implementation of SEVIS, the fact that SEVIS

15. Hartle, Terry W. Testimony before Committee on the Judiciary Subcommittee on Immigration, Border Security, and Claims. 18 September 2002.

16. "INS Releases Legal Status of Alleged Hijackers." CNN News. ⟨http://archives.cnn.com/2001/US/ 10/11/inv.ins.hijackers/index.html⟩. 11 October 2001.

is handled by Investigations and Customs Enforcement (ICE), and the general increased scrutiny of students illustrates that the government views students as a group that needs to be kept under observation. While one may question whether students pose as great a threat to the American people as the U.S. government's actions would indicate, other nonimmigrant groups are virtually ignored.

If security is the reasoning behind the attention that international students are receiving in regards to immigration laws implemented in the wake of terrorist acts, then one must ask why the policies are so inconsistent and why they virtually ignore other noncitizens entering the United States.

Never before had schools, including universities, flight schools, language schools, and any other school in the United States that accepts foreign students, been required to keep such close tabs on the international students they enroll. Nor had these institutions played such an important role for the INS and Department of State. But, as Doris Meissner, former commissioner for the INS, pointed out, "The September 11 terrorists were foreign visitors. They were here with validly issued visas, including student visas. And so it was inevitable that in the national response to September 11 there would be efforts made to tighten immigration controls."[18]

A database to track foreign students in the United States was the focus of much discussion throughout the mid- to late-1990s, with predecessors like CIPRIS and ISEAS. It was the USA PATRIOT Act, developed shortly after the 9/11 attacks, that mandated that a permanent tracking system, which would be known as the Student and Exchange Visitor Information System, or SEVIS, be implemented by January 1, 2003. In §416, the USA PATRIOT Act states:[19]

---

17. Beccar Varela, Jeronimo. Personal interview with author. 30 July 2004.
18. Meissner, Doris. Statement Before the National Press Club Policy Forum. 14 July 2003.
19. HR 3162 RDS. USA PATRIOT Act. §416. 24 October 2001.

SEC. 416. FOREIGN STUDENT MONITORING PROGRAM.

(a) Full Implementation and Expansion of Foreign Student Visa Monitoring Program Required.

The Attorney General, in consultation with the Secretary of State, shall fully implement and expand the program established by section 641(a) of the Illegal Immigration Reform and Immigrant Responsibility Act of 1996 (8 U.S.C. 1372(a).

(b) Integration With Port of Entry Information.

For each alien with respect to whom information is collected under section 641 of the Illegal Immigration Reform and Immigrant Responsibility Act of 1996 (8 U.S.C. 1372), the Attorney General, in consultation with the Secretary of State, shall include information on the date of entry and port of entry.

(c) Expansion of System To Include Other Approved Educational Institutions.

Section 641 of the Illegal Immigration Reform and Immigrant Responsibility Act of 1996 (8 U.S.C.1372) is amended —
(1) in subsection (a)(1), subsection (c)(4)(A), and subsection (d)(1) (in the text above subparagraph (A)), by inserting, "other approved educational institutions," after "higher education" each place it appears;
(2) in subsections (c)(1)(C), (c)(1)(D), and (d)(1)(A), by inserting, "or other approved educational institution," after "higher education" each place it appears;
(3) in subsections (d)(2), (e)(1), and (e)(2), by inserting, "other approved educational institution," after "higher education" each place it appears; and
(4) in subsection (h), by adding at the end the following new paragraph: "(3) Other approved educational institution. — The term 'other approved educational institution' includes any air flight school, language training school, or vocational school, approved by the Attorney General, in consultation with the Secretary of Education and the Secretary of State,

under subparagraph (F), (J), or (M) of section 101(a)(15) of the Immigration and Nationality Act."

(d) Authorization of Appropriations.

There is authorized to be appropriated to the Department of Justice $36,800,000 for the period beginning on the date of enactment of this Act and ending on January 1, 2003, to fully implement and expand prior to January 1, 2003, the program established by section 641(a) of the Illegal Immigration Reform and Immigrant Responsibility Act of 1996 (8 U.S.C. 1372(a).

After the events of 9/11, the American public was left to ask how something that catastrophic could occur within the United States. Attention was directed to the question of how the terrorists were able to enter the country. Adding fuel to the fire was the miscommunication that occurred between the INS and a contracted company, Affiliated Computer Services,[20] that notified applicants of change of status approvals. Six months after September 11, Mohammed Atta and Marwan Al-Shehhi were mailed their approval notices and were sent student visas, much to the outrage of the President and the American people. Deputy Press Secretary, Scott McClellan stated, on behalf of the President, "The president is very displeased. He wants to know how and why it happened and wants it fixed. The president has directed Governor Ridge to work with the attorney general and get to the bottom of this immediately. This is unacceptable."[21] Change was in the air, and it would be students who would bear the brunt of these changes.

After 9/11 it became apparent that it was a challenge to balance both the needs and benefits of international education with the threat of terrorism that foreign students were perceived to bring to the United States. It was Representative Phil Gingrey (R-Georgia)

---

20. "INS Chief Blames Visa Mess on Old Technology." CNN News. ‹http://archives.cnn.com/2002/ALLPOLITICS/03/19/ins.visa.mess/index.html›. 20 March 2002.

21. Garrett, Major. "Bush Upset By INS Visas to Hijackers, Aide Says." CNN News. ‹http://archives.cnn.com/2002/ALLPOLITICS/03/13/Bush.INS/index.html›. 13 March 2002.

who reminded educators that "keeping an open door to international students now must take a back seat to national security,"[22] while Secretary of State Colin Powell reiterated that international education "encourages and sustains democratic practices, creates a cohort of future leaders who understand each other's countries from the inside, and promotes long-term linkages between institutions here and abroad."[23] The reality of the politics surrounding international education and terrorism draws into question whether the United States can maintain a "Secure Borders, Open Doors"[24] policy when terrorism seems an ominous threat.

One of the steps the United States took to strengthen the security of the country was to implement SEVIS. While a system such as SEVIS was in the works long before 9/11, the events of that day created an increased urgency to have the SEVIS system fully implemented and functional. The government recognized the need to welcome international students and scholars into the country; largely because of the positive economic impact foreign students have on the country. Failure to welcome these individuals would have a long-term detrimental effect on the United States. As Colin Powell expressed in an op-ed piece in the *Wall Street Journal*, "When a foreign student goes elsewhere to school, we lose not only the student, but his entire family, including siblings, who might have followed in their brother's or sister's footsteps."[25]

SEVIS may allow students and exchange visitors to enter the United States, albeit under increased scrutiny and tighter regulations; however, many within the international community believe that the system contradicts the "essential, embracing spirit of America"[26] that the Secure Borders, Open Doors policy hopes to

---

22. Arnone, Michael. "College Officials Urge Lawmakers to Fix Problems That Security Measures Pose for Foreign Students." The Chronicle. 27 March 2003.

23. Ward, David. Testimony Before U.S. House of Representatives Committee on the Judiciary Subcommittee on Immigration, Border Security, and Claims. 2 April 2003.

24. Powell, Colin. "Remarks on Securing the Future of Travel and Tourism at the Second Annual Summit of the U.S. Chamber of Commerce." 12 May 2004.

25. Powell, Colin. "Secure Borders, Open Doors." *The Wall Street Journal*. 21 April 2004.

26. *Ibid.*

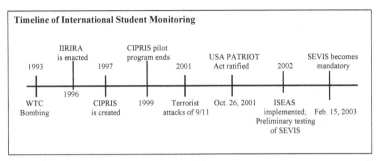

Timeline of International Student Monitoring

preserve. As Louis Meucci, advisor at Showa Boston Institute, made clear, "I almost feel like we're supposed to scare students, whereas before we informed them and they made their choices, but now it's like they're supposed to be just scared to do the wrong thing lest they be perceived as a terrorist and be sent out of the United States and never be allowed to come back."

Having become mandatory on February 15, 2003, the full use of the database was delayed from its original debut date of January 30, 2003 because many schools, including Harvard University, had not yet received their approval to use SEVIS from the INS.[27] Even with the slight delay, many felt that the timing was not appropriate for the system to become mandatory. Glenn Fine, Inspector General of the Department of Justice, stated at a subcommittee hearing September 18, 2002, "We continue to believe that full implementation of SEVIS is unlikely by the deadline of January 30, 2003."[28]

Contributing to the feelings that SEVIS would not be ready in January 2003 was the fact that there were several steps involved before approval to use SEVIS could be granted. Each of the nearly 6,000 schools that accepted foreign students had to be approved before theyb could use SEVIS. The approval process was long and tedious for both the school and the INS. Independent contractors were hired to carry out the thousands of inspections to be

---

27. Bombardieri, Marcella. "Paying Security's Price." *The Boston Globe* 10 February 2003: B5.

28. Fine, Glenn. "Select Education Subcommittee Hearing" 24 September 2002.

completed before the January 30, 2003 deadline. Many of the contractors had no experience with immigration and needed assistance from the schools to explain what, indeed, they were looking at during the inspection. School officials and the contractors themselves expressed concern over the preparedness of the inspection staff. Virga Mohsini, director of international student affairs at Emerson College, recalls a conversation she had with an inspector, who claimed he had "a very short briefing in terms of training."[29] While the INS provided inspectors with a checklist of what to look for during the inspection process, many felt that the inspectors were not knowledgeable enough about student immigration policies to spot a problem, should there be one.

The certification process began with schools and sponsoring agencies completing and submitting the Form I-17 by November 15, 2002. To defray the costs of the inspections, schools were charged $230 as a fee for processing the Form I-17, as well as a $350 fee for the on-site visit. Institutions that agreed to enroll in the preliminary version of SEVIS were exempt from having a site visit prior to the January 30, 2003 deadline, although the INS stated that site visits would be conducted later in the year.[30] With the exception of the trial schools, all other schools that admitted foreign students were to have been inspected by a contracted INS official before the January 30 deadline.

In reality, not all schools were inspected by the January 30, 2003 deadline, and the INS was forced to extend the deadline to February 15; and while preliminary schools were not required to complete the certification process by the deadline, many of the schools waited quite long before being inspected.

To assist the schools with the on-site visits, a "contractor checklist" began circulating in the international education community listing many of the things the inspector for the INS

---

29. Mohsini, Virga. Personal interview with author. 7 May 2004.

30. United States. "Preliminary Enrollment in the Student and Exchange Visitor Information System." U.S. Immigration and Naturalization Service. Washington, 2 July 2002.

would be looking for at the site visit.[31] Developed by the University of Georgia, the checklist was created to guide schools through the inspection process. In addition to listing the items that should be found in the student files requested by the INS, the checklist included information such as the school's immigration-related procedures, evidence of accreditation, and proof that the facility is a school. Although the checklist was helpful, many schools had very different experiences when inspection time arrived. Some schools reported that the inspector stayed less than an hour, hardly even opening the packet of information that the school officials had so laboriously prepared for months, while other schools reported having an intensive review of their records and facilities.

Many school officials questioned the qualifications and preparedness of the contracted inspectors. One school official said that the inspector who came to her school stated, "immigration is not my line of specialization."[32] Another school official did not believe that the contractor who performed the site visit at his school would have been able to recognize any problems or irregularities, should there be any. He said, "I talked to her, she was very pleasant, professional, but clueless and I don't think would have the intuition to know if we are a good school or if something suspect is going on."[33]

In addition to the potential inexperience of the contractors, other problems with the certification process raise questions as to whether or not the site review/certification process is accomplishing the first part of its stated goal of "balancing the security of the homeland with facilitating the entry of legitimate foreign students and exchange visitors."[34] Although the intentions of such a certification process have beneficial potential, that

---

31. "Contractor Checklist." University of Georgia. ⟨http://www.uga.edu/gaie/site-visit.doc⟩. 1 November 2002.

32. Mohsini, Virga. Personal interview with author. 7 May 2004.

33. Meucci, Louis. Personal interview with author. 12 May 2004.

34. Drury, Jill. "Memorandum for Academic Institutions That Are Not Currently SEVIS Certified." U.S. Department of Homeland Security. Washington, 25 July 2003.

potential will not be reached if those who are charged with carrying out the on-site visits do not have a complete understanding of the immigration processes required of schools and agencies sponsoring exchange visitors.

One glaring loophole within the certification process is that the INS in many cases sent the school the names of the files that would be reviewed, prior to the site visit. Presumably, the files requested by the INS were on students that the INS already knew were supposed to be attending that school. This is not necessarily problematic *per se*; however, this method would not alert the INS to any potential disputable practices that the school might be engaged in, such as permitting individuals to study at their institutions when they might not be legally allowed to do so. Perhaps it would be more beneficial for the INS to review files at random during the site visit to check for compliance.

This also brings up the question of what actions are taken should violations be found during the certification process. What are the consequences of not having complete files on the students or not meeting the criteria of the certification process? Though information regarding which schools were denied SEVIS certification has not been made public, it is believed that the majority of those schools were flight-training facilities. Of the thousands of colleges, universities, English-language schools, vocational training programs and sponsoring agencies that had a site visit, only a handful were denied SEVIS certification; however, there were other schools that did not provide all the requested materials during the certification process, such as not having I-20s on file for some students, and they were eventually approved.

Although time consuming and potentially costly, it may be beneficial for schools that do not initially meet the criteria for the on-campus site reviews to be given a warning and then reinspected within six months. It seems counterproductive to allow schools with questionable recordkeeping or admissions practices to be SEVIS certified, assuming the inspector is able to recognize any inconsistencies or problems.

While there may be a few schools whose certification to use SEVIS may be debatable, the vast majority of SEVIS certified schools are making every effort to comply with the SEVIS regulations. Many schools are struggling, however, with their extended role within the government under SEVIS. As one article stated, "the greatest irony of SEVIS may be that the program has forced the very school officials most leery of efforts to monitor students to take on that role on the government's behalf."[35] Schools frustrated by the policing they must now do as part of their international student advising jobs are finding it difficult to balance the responsibility of being welcoming to students at their institutions with their responsibilities to SEVIS and the U.S. government.

The SEVIS system itself largely dictates what information must be entered, thus eliminating some of the confusion that was present before the system was in place. Confusion still occurs as to how to report situations that are not clearly defined in the regulations. Initially, the SEVIS helpdesk, often a school's only contact with the government to clarify SEVIS issues, was run by inexperienced contracted employees who were more knowledgeable about the technical issues than the regulatory issues of SEVIS. Though the assistance of the helpdesk has improved dramatically since its inception, with more knowledgeable people staffing the phone lines and shorter wait times, issues of clarity still remain.

The final SEVIS regulatory notice was published on December 12, 2002, a little over a month before SEVIS became mandatory. The Senior Vice President of the American Council on Education, Terry W. Hartle, expressed frustration with this lack of guidance prior to full SEVIS implementation at a subcommittee hearing before the House in September 2002.[36] Without regulatory guidance and clarification, schools are dependent on their interpretation of the law, and can only hope that their understanding (or lack thereof)

35. Harris, Shane. "Watch Out." *Government Executive Magazine.* 15 July 2003.
36. Hartle, Terry W. Testimony before Committee on the Judiciary Subcommittee on Immigration, Border Security, and Claims. 18 September 2002.

will not have a detrimental effect on their students or exchange visitors. Organizations such as NAFSA have regular phone conferences with government officials in an effort to gain clarification on pressing issues. Scott Quint, director of the international student office at Northeastern University, said in an interview, "It's not all bad, but we need some level of clarity. If a student does something that inadvertently violates her status, it's not as repairable as it used to be."[37]

In addition to a lack of clearly defined regulations regarding student and exchange visitors, SEVIS users have had to contend with many technical problems. At first, the system was fraught with problems which frustrated users and dampened their confidence in the system. Schools reported that they were having "slow, spotty access to the system; data get lost or erased; and forms can't be printed out or show information from an entirely different institution."[38] The technical problems were part of the cause for the delay that moved the mandatory SEVIS deadline from January 30 to February 15, 2003. As INS spokesman Chris Bently explained, "There were certainly indications there were problems that were cropping up. This is a way to afford those schools two more weeks to work through those issues."[39] Furthermore, in some instances data that was input into SEVIS was not being transmitted to the consulates, and that delayed visa issuance for some candidates. This was discussed by David Ward, President of the American Council on Education, before a House subcommittee meeting,[40]

> Some embassies and consulates find that it takes a week or longer for them to access data entered into SEVIS. This means that students arrive at an embassy — sometimes after traveling a great

---

37. Bombardieri, Marcella. "Colleges Fault System to Track Foreign Students." *Boston Globe.* 30 January 2003.

38. Arnone, Michael. "Federal Foreign-Student Database Is Not Fully Used at U.S. Borders." *Chronicle of Higher Education.* 23 April 2004.

39. Sainz, Adrian. "INS Extends Deadline for Foreign Student Tracking System." *Boston Globe.* 30 January 2003.

40. Ward, David. Testimony Before U.S. House of Representatives Committee on the Judiciary Subcommittee on Immigration, Border Security, and Claims. 2 April 2003.

distance — only to be told (incorrectly) that their data has not been entered into SEVIS and that they may not apply for a visa. In fact, their data is in SEVIS — that's the only way they would received an I-20 form.

Debbie Nanni of Tufts University points out that such glitches were to be expected. "Given the magnitude of the task and the number of schools and people involved, the glitches, while frustrating, should not detract from the significant progress that has occurred and continues to occur."[41]

What is more worrisome is the consequences of errors made in SEVIS. At least initially, with all data being put into the system by hand, the potential for human error was very real, with very serious consequences for the student or exchange visitor. Advisors' fears were realized when an international student from Southeastern University was arrested because of an error in SEVIS.[42] And while this case is the extreme, it remains difficult to fix errors made within the system. If an error is discovered, whether that inaccuracy is the product of incorrect data input or a glitch in the SEVIS system itself, a formal request must be made to the SEVIS helpdesk to alleviate the problem. After a ticket number is obtained from the helpdesk, the process of receiving a "data fix" can begin. Information and documents must then be faxed to the SEVIS helpdesk. Currently it takes approximately two months for the error to be corrected by the government, a waiting period that can be very burdensome for students, particularly if they need to travel. And, it is not inconceivable for a data fix to take upwards of six months before a resolution.

Also frustrating are the government's inconsistencies in regard to student visa regulations. Students who apply for optional practical training (OPT) are required to do so before graduation, yet some schools have had students apply for OPT months after

---

41. Timerman, Jordana. "Tufts to Use Government Program to Track International Students." *The Tufts Daily.* 28 April 2003.

42. Becker, Robert. "Glitches Riddle Database to Track Foreign Students." *Chicago Tribune.* 17 March 2003.

graduation. The students are authorized by the government, contrary to what regulations state. Furthermore, students who initially enter on an I-20 are only to be admitted into the United States thirty days before the start of their program, yet a student was recently admitted more than ninety days before the program start date. Discrepancies such as these are discouraging not only because they are divergent to what the regulations say, but also because it makes advisors, who counsel international students as to the regulations, are made to appear unknowledgeable and overbearing.

For all the emphasis that the government has placed on the SEVIS database, the system will work only as well as those monitoring it. It is one thing to ensure that school officials enter information into the system, but it is another to ensure that the system is checked and utilized regularly by the government; if it is not, then it becomes a moot operation that does little to prevent terrorism. The doubts that many in the academic community had regarding the government's ability to monitor such a database were articulated when *The Chronicle of Higher Education* interviewed Jill Drury, director of SEVP. "The primary line of customs officers that foreign students encounter at airports, seaports, and border crossings currently does not have direct access to the Student and Exchange Visitor Information System, or SEVIS," she noted.[43] When immigration officers who are the first line of defense in the war on terrorism are not only do not check SEVIS, they do not even have access to it, significant questions arise as to the seriousness the government places on SEVIS and its potential ability to avert terrorism. It wasn't until June 2004, some two years after the implementation of SEVIS, that CBP officers had some access to the SEVIS database, and even then it was not full access. The records of students who had been terminated in the system were flagged, as an

---

43. Arnone, Michael. "Customs Officials Gain Access to Database." *Chronicle of Higher Education.* 4 June 2004.

indicator that should alert immigration officers to provide closer inspection of the student before admitting them into the U.S.[44]

ACRONYMS IN THE EDUCATIONAL FIELD

NAFSA: Association of International Educators — provides guidance and interpretation of immigration regulations to those in the international education community

NASFAA — National Association of Student Financial Aid Administrators

AACRAO — American Association of Collegiate Registrars and Admissions Officers

IEP — Intensive English Programs

IIE — Institute of International Education

Monitoring of the system remains in question; but the impact of SEVIS and the tighter laws governing international students have already had a huge impact on enrollment at schools within the United States.

Colleges and universities had seen a steady increase in the number of international students attending, however, the 2002-2003 academic year saw one of the smallest increases in recent times — less than one percent.[45] The 2002-2003 academic year was the first to be fully impacted by the events of 9/11 (presumably, most students enrolled in the 2001-2002 year were already present in the country prior to the terrorist attacks and statistics from that year do not include students who left the country after the attacks).

The 2004 Open Doors Report conducted by the Institute of International Education (IIE), an organization that promotes international educational exchange, shows the first decrease in the number of international students coming to the United States to

---

44. *Ibid.*

45. "Open Doors 2003: Report on International Education Exchange, 2003." Hey-Kyung Koh Chin, ed. New York: Institute of International Education.

study at institutions of higher education since 9/11. While English language programs have seen significant drops in enrollment, and colleges and universities have sometimes seen minimal growth in their international student populations, 2004 marked the first time since 1972 that there was an actual decline.[46] The Open Doors Report shows an overall drop of 2.4%, with undergraduate enrollment dropping nearly 5% (though graduate enrollment increased by 2.5%).[47]

With international education contributing $12.9 billion to the U.S. economy each year, slow growth can hurt.[48] This, combined with the fact that many international student offices at colleges and universities have had to hire additional staff, invest in software, and put in more hours to maintain accurate records in the SEVIS database to monitor their charges, has led to increased operating costs. As one school official noted, "It's at a time when we're having to say to the people at the top, 'oh, and I need several thousand or tens of thousands for software and I need another staff and I need to go to more conferences' and it's more expensive at a time when enrollment is significantly dropping."[49]

LAWS GOVERNING INTERNATIONAL STUDENTS

IIRIRA — Illegal Immigration Reform and Immigrant Responsibility Act of 1996

IIRIRA §641 — The section of IIRIRA that mandates a national database to track foreign students

USA PATRIOT Act — Uniting and Strengthening America by Providing Appropriate Tools Required to Intercept and Obstruct Terrorism Act of 2001

---

46. "Open Doors 2004: Report on International Education Exchange, 2004." Hey-Kyung Koh Chin, ed. New York: Institute of International Education.
47. *Ibid.*
48. "Open Doors 2003: Report on International Education Exchange, 2003." Hey-Kyung Koh Chin, ed. New York: Institute of International Education.
49. Meucci, Louis. Personal interview with author. 12 May 2004.

USA PATRIOT Act $416 — Section of Act that outlines the implementation of a foreign student tracking system

FERPA — Family Educational Rights and Privacy Act

USA PATRIOT Act $507 — Section of Act that amends FERPA and allows for ex parte disclosure of student records to the U.S. government

On top of the added costs international student offices were now faccing, there were also sweeping changes in the Family Educational Rights and Privacy Act (FERPA) under the USA PATRIOT Act. Under FERPA, schools are ineligible to receive federal money if they have a policy of disclosing students' personal information or educational records without written consent from the parent or student (though there are exceptions to this). The USA PATRIOT Act added a new exception, allowing schools to release information about students. As noted in a letter written by LeRoy S. Rooker, Director of the Family Policy Compliance Office of the U.S. Department of Education:[50]

> The recent amendment to FERPA permits educational agencies and institutions to disclose — without the consent or knowledge of the student or parent — personally identifiable information from the student's education records to the Attorney General of the United States or to his designee in response to an *ex parte* order in connection with the investigation or prosecution of terrorism crimes.

FERPA has been a foundation of the educational system since its creation in 1974. This Act protects the rights and privacy of students, however, with the USA PATRIOT Act, it has become easier for that information to be released. $507 of the USA PATRIOT Act reads:

---

50. Rooker, LeRoy S. Letter to education colleagues. 12 April 2002.

SEC. 507. DISCLOSURE OF EDUCATIONAL RECORDS.

SECTION 444 OF THE GENERAL EDUCATION PROVISIONS ACT (20 U.S.C. 1232G), IS AMENDED BY ADDING AFTER SUBSEC-TION (I) A NEW SUBSECTION (J) TO READ AS FOLLOWS:

(j) INVESTIGATION AND PROSECUTION OF TERRORISM

(1) IN GENERAL — Notwithstanding subsections (a) through (i) or any provision of State law, the Attorney General (or any Federal officer or employee, in a position not lower than an Assistant Attorney General, desig-nated by the Attorney General) may submit a written application to a court of competent jurisdiction for an *ex parte* order requiring an educational agency or institution to permit the Attorney General (or his designee) to —

(A) collect education records in the possession of the educational agency or institution that are relevant to an authorized investigation or prosecution of an offense listed in section 2332b(g)(5)(B) of title 18 United States Code, or an act of domestic or international terrorism as defined in section 2331 of that title; and

(B) for official purposes related to the investigation or prosecution of an offense described in paragraph (1)(A), retain, disseminate, and use (including as evidence at trial or in other administrative or judicial proceedings) such records, consistent with such guidelines as the Attorney General, after consultation with the Secretary, shall issue to protect confidentiality.

(2) APPLICATION AND APPROVAL —

(A) In General — An application under paragraph (1) shall certify that there are specific and articulable facts giving reason to believe that the education records are likely to contain information described in paragraph (1)(A).

(B) The court shall issue an order described in paragraph (1) if the court finds that the application for the order includes the certification described in subparagraph (A).

(3) Protection of Educational Agency or Institution — An educational agency or institution that, in good faith,

produces education records in accordance with an order issued under this subsection shall not be liable to any person for that production.

(4) Record Keeping — Subsection (b)(4) does not apply to education records subject to a court order under this subsection.

Several of the items that must be released into SEVIS such as educational status, disciplinary action, and medical circumstances that may prevent a student from studying full-time were protected under FERPA prior to the enactment of the USA PATRIOT Act, an Act that states that information is to be released for the reason of "Investigation and Persecution of Terrorism." This implies that the government in large part views students as potential terrorist threats, a perception which is of course inaccurate in most cases. It is understandable that the government would want to easily access the personal information of students who are suspected of terrorist activity; however, such broad coverage is worrisome for all students and all Americans in general. Section 507 of the USA PATRIOT Act applies to all students, not just to international students. That this information is readily available to the government *ex parte* means that students need not be told of the inquiry into their records by the government, nor does written consent from the student need to be provided. As a statement from NASFA explains, "When the school makes a disclosure pursuant to an *ex parte* order, the school official is not required to record that disclosure of information in the student's file."[51]

The same applies to English Language (ESL) schools, which in particular have been negatively impacted by the increased scrutiny since the terrorist attacks of 2001. While colleges and universities have seen minimal increases in their enrollment of international students, English language schools have seen considerable declines in enrollment, in some cases as much as fifty percent. The intensified attention given to ESL schools is partly due to the fact that Hani

51. McCarthy, Karen. "USA PATRIOT Act Results in Amendments to FERPA; NASFAA Training Materials Updated." 12 June 2002.

Hanjour entered the United States on an I-20 from ELS Language Center, located on the campus of Holy Names College in Oakland, CA. The center that has since closed. It should be noted, however, that he had also entered the United States some years prior to 9/11 on a student visa from a different educational facility. Additionally, as illustrated by Hani Hanjour's case, it is more common for ESL students than to enter the country on a student visa and fail to show up for classes. According to the *Boston Globe*, "At two different local language schools, officials said that about one in twenty of the students they sponsor for visas fails to turn up for class."[52] A five-percent no show rate is disconcerting, given the history and the climate of terrorism in the country since September 11.

Furthermore, particularly with language schools, the quality of the schools can vary greatly. Some prepare students for a university education, while others market themselves as a fun opportunity for young internationals, emphasizing the entertainment and tourist attractions in close proximity to the school. This has led to increased visa denials for English language students and a higher level of inquiry once they are in the United States. As State Department spokesman Stuart Patt said in an article about the lower enrollments in English language schools post 9/11, "There are English language schools in Brazil. Why someone needs to come to the United States is unclear."[53]

Since September 11, there has been a perception that the United States is no longer a safe place. In addition to the economic weakness across the globe, the antipathy shared by many people throughout the world for recent U.S. political initiatives, and a disinclination to subject themselves to the hassle of more onerous visa application and security procedures in order to come to the U.S. for a short term program, many potential ESL students think twice about coming to the U.S. Through its immigration policies the U.S. has sent the message that international students are a group of

---

52. Bombardieri, Marcella. "Paying Security's Price." *Boston Globe*. 10 February 2003.
53. *Ibid.*

people that need to be watched, a message that is neither accurate nor welcoming, and it is one of several reasons that have contributed to lower numbers of international students, particularly among those seeking primarily to obtain English language skills. One student articulated this sentiment, saying,"I don't believe the scrutiny international students have received recently is just or fair."[54]

In turn, many ESL schools have eased their requirements for entering the school, and many will accept internationals whom they are mandated by law not to accept for full time study. Some permit tourists to enter the country for the sole purpose of studying. Banking on the fact that ICE will never discover this prohibited practice, to this day many of these schools continue to accept tourists and others on visa waivers. Unless ICE goes through each of the school's records, or if someone privy to the admission information for that school reports the institution, ICE has no way of tracking tourists or those on visa waivers to a particular school.

The declining enrollment at ESL schools has prompted heavy lobbying among the Intensive English Program (IEP) network, urging Congress to lighten the burden on students of short-term programs. Among other things they urge that tourists be allowed to study full-time at short term English language programs and that the SEVIS fee be reduced to $35 for ESL students. Discussion has also been given to developing a new student visa category, such as an F-4, for students of short-term programs. In a letter written by NAFSA colleagues, IEP school officials suggested that, "students enrolled at IEPs should be able to enter the country in tourist status rather than with an F-1 student visa. Until they can be reclassified, they should pay a reduced SEVIS fee of $35."[55] Officials of IEPs, such as Beata Schmid, Director of EF International Language Schools' Boston center, have been working in conjunction with Rep. Barney Frank (D-Mass.) to push such legislation through Congress.

---

54. Aragon Tello, Ana. Personal interview with author. 3 August 2004.
55. NAFSA News. 17 May 2004.

The fee, mandated under IIRIRA, "is to cover the costs for the continued operation of the Student and Exchange Visitor Program (SEVP) including the administration and maintenance of SEVIS, compliance activities, and the establishment of SEVIS Liaison Officers."[56] The final fee rules were not published until July 1, 2004, leaving schools two months to decide how the $100 fee should be collected. Because the "DHS will not be able to establish a workable arrangement for fee collection by DOS prior to the effective date of this rule,"[57] students and exchange visitors are required to pay the SEVIS fee via mail, the Internet, Western Union, or through the school in which the student intends to study. This method of payment is troubling for many schools; in the words of ACE's president, David Ward, "this approach will make it more difficult for foreign students, scholars, and exchange visitors to come to the United States."[58]

Concerns include the inability for some students to access the Internet or a credit card to pay the fee, the potential for delays and misplacements of payments by mail, and the potential financial liability for schools who pay the fee for their students.

There is no question that the legislation of recent years has had dramatic effects not only on English language schools, but also on international education in general within the United States. Through the implementation of SEVIS, international students and exchange visitors have never been monitored more closely. It remains to be seen, however, if SEVIS will have the desired outcome of deterring or preventing terrorism through the monitoring of students — or if schools will be able to survive the reduction in enrollment. A balance has yet to be achieved between welcoming new students to this country and protecting the United States against foreign terrorists. The cross-cultural educational experience

---

56. Drury, Jill. "Memorandum for All Academic Institutions and Program Sponsors." U.S. Department of Homeland Security. Washington, 29 June 2004.

57. Federal Register. "Authorizing Collection of the Fee Levied on F, J, and M Nonimmigrant Classifications Under Public Law 104-208; SEVIS." 1 July 2004.

58. Ward, Peter. "See Fee Collection Update." NAFSA Listserve. 24 June 2004.

and the understanding and cooperation that are achieved through that partnership may be the best deterrent of terrorism the United States could invest in.

5. Refugees and Asylum Seekers

Refugees and asylees are perhaps those most in need of protection from the United States more so than any other group of immigrants coming to this country's shores. While the United States resettles more refugees than any other country working with the United Nation's High Commissioner of Refugees (UNHCR), the U.S.'s program is not without its flaws, and those imperfections were only exacerbated by the September 11 terrorist attacks.

It is important to begin with an understanding of who is a refugee. The definition of a refugee, as stated in the Immigration and Nationality Act §101(42)(a) and §101(42)(b) is based on the definition created under the 1951 UN Refugee Convention. This law states:

> (42) The term "refugee" means:
> (A) any person who is outside any country of such person's nationality or, in the case of a person having no nationality, is outside any country in which such person last habitually resided, and who is unable or unwilling to return to, and is unable or unwilling to avail himself or herself of the protection of, that country because of persecution or a well-founded fear of persecution on account of race, religion, nationality,

membership in a particular social group, or political opinion, or

(B) in such circumstances as the President after appropriate consultation (as defined in section 207(e) of this Act) may specify, any person who is within the country of such person's nationality or, in the case of a person having no nationality, within the country in which such person is habitually residing, and who is persecuted or who has a well-founded fear of persecution on account of race, religion, nationality, membership in a particular social group, or political opinion. The term "refugee" does not include any person who ordered, incited, assisted, or otherwise participated in the persecution of any person on account of race, religion, nationality, membership in a particular social group, or political opinion. For purposes of determinations under this Act, a person who has been forced to abort a pregnancy or to undergo involuntary sterilization, or who has been persecuted for failure or refusal to undergo such a procedure or for other resistance to a coercive population control program, shall be deemed to have been persecuted on account of political opinion, and a person who has a well founded fear that he or she will be forced to undergo such a procedure or subject to persecution for such failure, refusal, or resistance shall be deemed to have a well founded fear of persecution on account of political opinion.

This definition is far more restrictive than many people have understood it to be. The need to provide evidence of "a well-founded fear of persecution on account of race, religion, nationality, membership in a particular social group, or political opinion" can be difficult, particularly if one has fled from home with few possessions. In a report issued by the Bureau of Population, Refugees, and Migration (PRM) under the Department of State, this point was reiterated. "Some persons readily labeled refugees by the press and public cannot make this showing. That is, the popular conception of a refugee is more expansive than the legal definition. Quite understandably, the popular view tends to include anyone who has crossed a border because of real dangers in the home country, whatever their precise nature."[1]

The United States has a long history of resettling those in need. Resettlement programs began after World War I and assisted Europeans fleeing from the war.[2] Resettlement agencies such as the International Rescue Committee, one of the U.S.'s largest refugee-related NGOs began during World War II, with the assistance of Albert Einstein, to resettle Jews fleeing from the Nazi regime.[3] Shortly thereafter large groups of refugees from the Soviet Union also began resettling in the U.S. From the 1970s through the 1990s, the U.S. resettled thousands of people from Southeast Asia and the former Soviet Union.[4] Throughout this nation's history large groups of people from specific areas of the world have resettled in the U.S. Much of the resettlement during the 1990s was facilitated by the "Lautenberg Amendment" that required less evidence of refugee status from former Soviet Union and Indochinese nationals.[5] The provision, which came under the Foreign Operations Appropriations Act of 1990, required those individuals "to prove that they are members of a protected category with a credible, but not necessarily individual, fear of persecution."[6]

With the sunset of the Lautenberg Amendment in FY2002,[7] the landscape of the refugee resettlement program has changed. In prior years, the majority of resettled refugees came from a limited number of places. As explained by Secretary for Population,

---

1. Martin, David A. "The United States Refugee Admissions Program: Reforms for a New Era of Refugee Resettlement." U.S. Department of State. Washington: GPO, 2004.

2. "A Brief History of LIRS and U.S. Immigration Policy." Lutheran Immigration and Refugee Services. ‹http://www.lirs.org/who/history.htm›. 2004.

3. "History of the International Rescue Committee." International Rescue Committee.‹http://www.theirc.org/index.cfm/wwwID/125/topicID/67/locationID/0›. May 2003.

4. Dewey, Arthur. "Statement Before the Senate Committee on the Judiciary, Subcommittee on Immigration, Border Security, and Citizenship." 21 September 2004.

5. P.L. 101-167. FY 1990 Foreign Operations Appropriations Act. 21 November 1989.

6. Bruno, Andorra and Katherine Bush. "Refugee Admissions and Resettlement Policy." CRS Report for Congress. 22 January 2002.

7. P.L. 107-116. Departments of Labor Health and Human Services, Education, and Related Agencies Appropriations Act, 2002. 10 January 2002.

Refugees, and Migration Arthur Dewey, "Now, we process refugees — a few hundred or a few thousand at a time — in about forty-six locations and representing sixty nationalities."[8] In addition to increased security concerns, the proliferation of processing locations stems from the fact that refugees today are often found in smaller pockets scattered throughout the world, rather than in the few large groups seen in previous years. This has created a challenge for U.S. immigration officials who are required to interview each potential refugee to ensure that the individual qualifies for refugee status and has cleared all appropriate security checks.

The United States makes an effort to settle about half of all those referred by the UNHCR,[9] making the United States the country that allows the most refugees to permanently resettle on its shores. This commitment requires the cooperation of several departments and organizations and is a challenging feat, one that has grown increasingly difficult since 9/11. Much of the coordination surrounding the U.S. Refugee Resettlement program, including proposing refugee resettlement numbers for the following fiscal year, is carried out by the Bureau of Population, Refugees, and Migration (PRM) under the Department of State. Prior to the beginning of each fiscal year, this bureau issues a report to Congress outlining the proposed resettlement initiatives for the upcoming year. Additionally, this Bureau "administers and monitors U.S. contributions to international and non-governmental organizations to assist and protect refugees abroad."[10]

The U.S. government and more specifically PRM work closely with several NGOs. Currently, PRM provides some funding for ten agencies within the United States in an effort to aid in the resettlement of refugees.[11] These agencies help find housing for the refugees, provide job and language training, and offer cultural

8. *Ibid.*

9. Bruno, Andorra and Katherine Bush. "Refugee Admissions and Resettlement Policy." CRS Report for Congress. 22 January 2002.

10. Bureau of Population, Refugees, and Migration. ⟨http://www.state.gov/g/prm/⟩.

11. Bureau for Population, Migration, and Refugees. "FY 2005 Report to Congress."

orientation, among other services. The assistance that these agencies provide for refugees is vital.

Much of the work in determining who will be resettled in the U.S. is completed by the PRM and the Department of Homeland Security's Citizenship and Immigration Services (USCIS). Officials from USCIS are primarily responsible for the adjudication of refugee applications. Officers from the USCIS review application materials, interview the applicant, and determine if resettlement is warranted.

Perhaps one of the most pressing issues post 9/11 in regard to the processing of refugees overseas was the safety concern of the then-INS officers required to conduct overseas interviews of refugee applicants (this is now completed by USCIS officers). Because of the increased risk associated with being an entity of the U.S. government in areas of the world that are often turbulent, the concerns for immigration officials' safety is not unfounded. As David A. Martin points out in his report on the refugee admissions process, "DHS adjudications officers are there precisely to make decisions, some of which will be negative and will therefore create disaffection and anger among the surrounding population. In these settings, extra care about officer safety and security is thoroughly justified — indeed imperative."[12] As discussed in the PRM FY2005 Report to Congress, these security concerns continue to be pressing and have contributed to the closure of some overseas refugee processing locations since 9/11.[13]

In the aftermath of 9/11, refugee admissions to the United States were halted on October 1, 2001. A moratorium on admissions was declared, to allow a reevaluation of admissions procedures to ensure the safety of the INS employees working to admit the refugees overseas and to prevent fraudulent applicants from entering the country. It was not until the end of November that the resettlement program resumed, and the program has since admitted

---

12. Martin, David A. "The United States Refugee Admissions Program: Reforms for a New Era of Refugee Resettlement." U.S. Department of State. Washington: GPO, 2004.

13. Bureau for Population, Migration, and Refugees. "FY 2005 Report to Congress." U.S. Department of State. Washington, 2004.

numbers of refugees that fall considerably short of the proposed refugee ceilings.

Contributing to the cessation of refugee admissions to the U.S. was the delay in the FY2002 Presidential Determination of refugee admissions. The President issues this notice annually, usually after congressional consultations and under advisement from various agencies including the PRM. Though the fiscal year begins October 1, the Presidential Determination for FY2002 was not issued until November 21, 2001, nearly two months into the fiscal year. During that time, from October 1 until November 21, no refugees were admitted into the United States.[14]

It is also interesting to note that while refugees were not allowed to be admitted into the U.S. during this time period, even those whose applications had been adjudicated prior to 9/11, other foreign nationals were. This raises several fundamental questions regarding the U.S. resettlement program. Did the United States view refugees as potentially more dangerous or threatening than other noncitizens, such that they could not be admitted into the country until additional security procedures could be put into place? Were the security procedures for the admittance of refugees to the U.S. so essentially flawed that terrorists could enter the country, requiring the cessation of the program until additional security measures could be taken? As one NGO worker said, "Politically, it is not the right thing to do, letting foreign nationals into the country right now."[15]

UNHCR — United Nations High Commissioner for Refugees

PRM — Bureau of Population, Refugees, and Migration; operates under the Department of State and is responsible for coordi-

---

14. Bruno, Andorra and Katherine Bush. "Refugee Admissions and Resettlement Policy." CRS Report for Congress. 22 January 2002.

15. Anonymous. Personal interview with author. 11 June 2004.

nating the refugee resettlement program within the U.S., works closely with NGOs, the UNHCR, and the DHS.

IOM — International Organization for Migration; an international organization that works closely with the United States government in the refugee resettlement process by performing medical examinations of refugees prior to admittance to the U.S. and provides travel resources to the United States for refugees.

ORR — Office of Refugee Resettlement; an office under the Department of Health and Human Service with provides resettlement assistance for refugees such as medical services and cash assistance.

FY2001 refugee admissions statistics do not reflect the drastic changes that occurred after 9/11 because the federal fiscal year ends September 30; therefore, the majority of refugees admitted during FY2001 were admitted prior to the terrorist attack.

FY2002 painted a grim picture of admissions of refugee to the United States. Though the ceiling for refugee admissions was 70,000, which was already ten thousand less than the previous fiscal year, only 27,029 refugees were actually admitted during FY2002.

From the terrorist attack of 1993 to the fallout after 9/11, the admissions of refugees into the United States for FY 2002 were reduced by more than half. For FY1993, a ceiling of 142,000 refugees had been proposed for resettlement into this country. By 2002, that number had been reduced to 70,000, a rate that has remained steady for several years, though crises in places such as Sudan, Somalia, and Liberia have created tens of thousands of refugees. It has been argued that much of the reasoning behind the drastic decline in the U.S.'s admission of refugees is the inability for the United States to effectively implement security controls that both prevent terrorism and assist those in need of resettlement.[16]

---

16. Kuck, Charles. Statement Before the Senate Judiciary Subcommittee on Immigration, Border Security, and Citizenship. 9 September 2004.

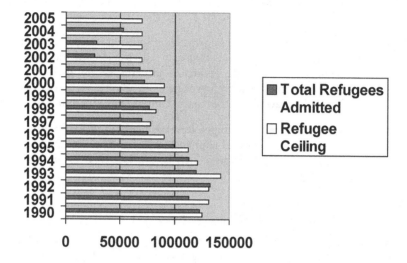

FIGURE 1: REFUGEE CEILINGS AND ADMISSIONS 1990-2005[17]

The numbers of refugees the President has authorized to be admitted to the U.S. have steadily declined within the last decade. In 1991, the admission rate was well over 100,000,[18] while the FY2005 report to Congress recommends only 70,000 refugees to be admitted.[19] In FY2004, the resettlement program saw some recovery from the attacks of 9/11 with 52,875 refugees being resettled into the United States, an eighty-five percent increase in admissions from

17. Patrick, Erin. "The US Refugee Resettlement Program." Migration Policy Institute. ‹http://www.migrationinformation.org/USfocus/display.cfm?id=54›. 1 September 2002. Peters, Philip. "Refugee Admissions Remain Below Par, Needs Remain High." The Lexington Institute. ‹http://www.lexingtoninstitute.org/immigration/040226.asp›. 26 February 2004.

18. United States Committee for Refugees. "In the Aftermath of September 11: U.S. Refugee Resettlement on Hold." *Worldwide Refugee Information Refugee Reports.* 22(9/10). September/October 2001.

19. Bureau for Population, Migration, and Refugees. "FY 2005 Report to Congress." U.S. Department of State. Washington, 2004.

the previous fiscal year.[20] PRM contributes this increase to "extraordinary efforts and coordination among federal agencies, international and non-governmental organizations, and overseas partners in successfully implementing and streamlining enhanced security requirements following September 11, 2001."[21] Though there was a significant increase in admissions numbers, a commendable effort for all agencies and organizations involved, the number still fell short of the proposed 70,000 admissions.

The attacks of 9/11 also prompted the review of security procedures in the admissions process. Following the attacks, the resettlement program within the United States completely stopped. As discussed in an article written by Bill Frelick for the U.S. Committee for Refugees, "The formal reason for the suspension of the resettlement program was to reassess its security components, but at various levels, all aspects of the program were under review."[22] This had both a detrimental and positive affect on the resettlement program. While many refugees were left in a state of limbo because they could not gain entry or be reviewed for refugee status, an assessment of the procedures surrounding the admission and security of the refugee resettlement program to the United States was necessary.

Among the changes implemented after the attacks of 9/11 was the USA PATRIOT Act, which deemed refugees inadmissible if they had had any association with a group that endorsed or supported terrorism. This amended the INA §212(a)(3)(B). Section 411 of the Act in part states:

---

20. Ereli, Adam. "Refugee Admissions for FY2004." Bureau of Population, Refugees, and Migration. 4 October 2004.

21. *Ibid.*

22. Felick, Bill. "Rethinking U.S. Refugee Admissions: Quantity and Quality." U.S. Committee for Refugees. 2002.

SEC. 411. DEFINITIONS RELATING TO TERRORISM.

(a) Grounds of Inadmissibility — Section 212(a)(3) of the Immigration and Nationality Act (8 U.S.C. 1182(a)(3)) is amended —

(1) in subparagraph (B) —

(A) in clause (i) —

(i) by amending subclause (IV) to read as follows:

"(IV) is a representative (as defined in clause (v)) of —

(aa) a foreign terrorist organization, as designated by the Secretary of State under section 219, or

(bb) a political, social or other similar group whose public endorsement of acts of terrorist activity the Secretary of State has determined undermines United States efforts to reduce or eliminate terrorist activities";

(ii) in subclause (V), by inserting "or" after "section 219"; and

(iii) by adding at the end the following new subclauses: "(VI) has used the alien's position of prominence within any country to endorse or espouse terrorist activity, or to persuade others to support terrorist activity or a terrorist organization, in a way that the Secretary of State has determined undermines United States efforts to reduce or eliminate terrorist activities," or "(VII) is the spouse or child of an alien who is inadmissible under this section, if the activity causing the alien to be found inadmissible occurred within the last 5 years";

(B) by redesignating clauses (ii), (iii), and (iv) as clauses (iii), (iv), and (v), respectively;

(C) in clause (i)(II), by striking "clause (iii)" and inserting "clause (iv)";

(D) by inserting after clause (i) the following:

(ii) EXCEPTION— Subclause (VII) of clause (i) does not apply to a spouse or child —

(I) who did not know or should not reasonably have known of the activity causing the alien to be found inadmissible under this section; or

(II) whom the consular officer or Attorney General has reasonable grounds to believe has renounced the activity causing the alien to be found inadmissible under this section";

(E) in clause (iii) (as redesignated by subparagraph (B)) —

(i) by inserting "it had been" before "committed in the United States"; and

(ii) in subclause (V)(b), by striking "or firearm" and inserting ", firearm, or other weapon or dangerous device";

(F) by amending clause (iv) (as redesignated by subparagraph (B)) to read as follows:

(iv) ENGAGE IN TERRORIST ACTIVITY DEFINED — As used in this chapter, the term "engage in terrorist activity" means, in an individual capacity or as a member of an organization —

(I) to commit or to incite to commit, under circumstances indicating an intention to cause death or serious bodily injury, a terrorist activity;

(II) to prepare or plan a terrorist activity;

(III) to gather information on potential targets for terrorist activity;

(IV) to solicit funds or other things of value for —

(aa) a terrorist activity;

(bb) a terrorist organization described in clause (vi)(I) or (vi)(II); or

(cc) a terrorist organization described in clause (vi)(III), unless the solicitor can demonstrate that he did not know, and should not reasonably have known, that the solicitation would further the organization's terrorist activity;

(V) to solicit any individual —

(aa) to engage in conduct otherwise described in this clause;

(bb) for membership in a terrorist organization described in clause (vi)(I) or (vi)(II); or

(cc) for membership in a terrorist organization described in clause (vi)(III), unless the solicitor can demonstrate that he did not know, and should not reasonably have known, that the solicitation would further the organization's terrorist activity; or

(VI) to commit an act that the actor knows, or reasonably should know, affords material support, including a safe house, transportation, communications, funds, transfer of funds or other material financial benefit, false documentation or identification, weapons (including chemical, biological, or radiological weapons), explosives, or training —

(aa) for the commission of a terrorist activity;

(bb) to any individual who the actor knows, or reasonably should know, has committed or plans to commit a terrorist activity;

(cc) to a terrorist organization descried in clause (vi)(I) or (vi)(II); or

(dd) to a terrorist organization described in clause (vi)(III), unless the actor can demonstrate that he did not know, and should not reasonably have known, that the act would further the organization's terrorist activity. This clause shall not apply to any material support the alien afforded to an organization or individual that has committed terrorist activity, if the Secretary of State, after consultation with the Attorney General, or the Attorney General, after consultation with the Secretary of State, concludes in his sole unreviewable discretion, that this clause should not apply; and

(G) by adding at the end the following new clause:

(vi) TERRORIST ORGANIZATION DEFINED — As used in clause (i)(VI) and clause (iv), the term "terrorist organization" means an organization —

(I) designated under section 219;

(II) otherwise designated, upon publication in the Federal Register, by the Secretary of State in consultation with or upon the request of the Attorney General, as a terrorist organization, after finding that the organization engages in the activities described in subclause (I), (II), or (III) of clause (iv), or that the organization provides material support to further terrorist activity; or

(III) that is a group of two or more individuals, whether organized or not, which engages in the activities described in subclause (I), (II), or (III) of clause (iv); and

(2) by adding at the end the following new subparagraph:

(F) ASSOCIATION WITH TERRORIST ORGANIZATIONS — Any alien who the Secretary of State, after consultation with the Attorney General, or the Attorney General, after consultation with the Secretary of State, determines has been associated with a terrorist organization and intends while in the United States to engage solely, principally, or incidentally in activities that could endanger the welfare, safety, or security of the United States is inadmissible.

(b) CONFORMING AMENDMENTS —

(1) Section 237(a)(4)(B) of the Immigration and Nationality Act (8 U.S.C. 1227(a)(4)(B)) is amended by striking "section 212(a)(3)(B)(iii)" and inserting "section 212(a)(3)(B)(iv)".

(2) Section 208(b)(2)(A)(v) of the Immigration and Nationality Act (8 U.S.C. 1158(b)(2)(A)(v)) is amended by striking "or (IV)" and inserting "(IV), or (VI)".

(c) RETROACTIVE APPLICATION OF AMENDMENTS —

(1) In General — Except as otherwise provided in this subsection, the amendments made by this section shall take effect on the date of the enactment of this Act and shall apply to —

(A) actions taken by an alien before, on, or after such date; and

(B) all aliens, without regard to the date of entry or attempted entry into the United States —

(i) in removal proceedings on or after such date (except for proceedings in which there has been a final administrative decision before such date); or

(ii) seeking admission to the United States on or after such date.

On the surface, this component of the USA PATRIOT Act appears to be an understandable and necessary feature in preventing terrorism, but it is fundamentally flawed, to the detriment of many refugees. This section fails to recognize that often, particularly in the case of those claiming refugee status, applicants are without choice in being associated with a group and may be claiming refugee status because parting from the group would result in persecution. To draw a line so distinctly without fully assessing the consequences or real-life application of such a provision is unrealistic.

Emphasis must be made on this point, particularly in the light of those seeking asylum in a foreign country. It is highly credible that a spouse or child would seek refugee status because of the actions of a spouse or parent; that affiliation could put them in grave danger and could be the very reasoning behind the desire to seek refuge in the first place. Section 411 does provide an exception to this in the case of spouses and children, namely that they did not know about the activities or they have renounced it. The same could be said for other relatives or family members, as well; yet the exception provided in the USA PATRIOT Act does not apply to them. In September 2004, at a Senate Subcommittee hearing, Charles Kuck stated, "National security, if that is the primary goal of our immigration system, is most effectively enhanced by improving the mechanisms for identifying actual terrorists, not by implementing harsher or unattainable standards or blindly treating all foreigners as potential terrorists."[23]

Steps have been taken since 9/11 in an effort to improve the refugee resettlement process, increase security, and reduce fraud. They include creating a database that holds information regarding refugee applications, increased staffing, additional funding, better cooperation between the departments and agencies within the U.S., the UNHCR, and NGOs, delegation of name check and Security

---

23. Kuck, Charles. Statement Before the Senate Judiciary Subcommittee on Immigration, Border Security, and Citizenship. 9 September 2004.

Advisory Opinion responsibilities to the Department of State, and implementing the Worldwide Refugee Admissions Processing System (WRAPS).[24] These efforts are necessary to improve the overall refugee assistance program and to ensure the increased safety of the people of the United States. And while 9/11 was in part the impetus to implement these policies and procedures, many of these changes are beneficial and perhaps should have been considered and employed, anyway.

The execution of some of these new measures has not, however, always been smooth. As with other areas of immigration policy, communication between the different offices of the Department of Homeland Security has not always been effective. This point was discussed in a report conducted for the Department of State by David A. Martin, reviewing the refugee resettlement program of the United States. He writes, "Some such central monitoring, coordination, and oversight capacity for immigration policy, probably attached to either the Secretary's or the Deputy Secretary's office, is highly necessary, especially given that immigration responsibilities formerly under the unified responsibility of the Commissioner of INS are now split among three separate bureaus."[25] As Martin makes note, most delays are caused by the competing interests of enforcement, under ICE and services, under the USCIS.[26]

Dividing the responsibilities of the INS, as discussed more thoroughly in Chapter 2, was intended to create a system that was more efficient and worked to better protect the country by reducing oversights and mistakes, yet the division has instead largely created a lack of communication between the bureaus, increased delays, and fostered confusion.[27]

---

24. "U.S. Government to Expedite Refugee Processing Since September 11, 2001." U.S. Department of State. Washington, 18 July 2003.

25. Martin, David A. "The United States Refugee Admissions Program: Reforms for a New Era of Refugee Resettlement." U.S. Department of State. Washington: GPO, 2004.

26. *Ibid.*

27. "Ashcroft Back House Bill to Split up INS." CNN News. ⟨http://archives.cnn.com/ 2002/LAW/04/25/ ins.ashcroft/index.html⟩. 25 April 2002.

As September 11 illustrated, the refugee resettlement program of the United States' has a "vulnerability to unforeseen problems,"[28] thus affecting admission numbers and more importantly the United States' ability to aid those who are fleeing persecution. Martin suggests the creation of a Refugee Committee, which would include members of the Department of State, the Department of Homeland Security, as well as representatives from the UNHCR, the International Organization of Migration, and NGOs.[29] Martin's suggestion is a commonsense approach to addressing the issues, particularly those post 9/11, relating to the refugee admissions to the United States. Without a coordinated method to admissions, it is unlikely that improvements will be made to benefit the security of the country or the resettlement program as a whole.

One task of the Refugee Committee suggested by Martin would be to revamp the current priority system that the United States employs when admitting refugees into the country. Like other aspects of immigration, refugee admissions are based on a priority system, with Priority 1 (P-1) referring to those cases submitted by the UNHCR, the U.S. Embassy, or NGOs, Priority 2 (P-2) referring to groups of "special humanitarian concern," and Priority 3 (P-3) referring to family reunification.[30] The P-1 category is largely based on criteria outlined by the UNHCR Resettlement Handbook, which gives P-1 resettlement consideration to refugees who may be subject to one or more of the following situations:[31]

- The threat of refoulement
- Threat of arrest or detention
- Threat to safety or human rights in the country in which they seek refuge

---

28. Martin, David A. "The United States Refugee Admissions Program: Reforms for a New Era of Refugee Resettlement." U.S. Department of State. Washington: GPO, 2004.
   29. *Ibid.*
   30. Bureau for Population, Migration, and Refugees. "FY 2005 Report to Congress." U.S. Department of State. Washington, 2004.
   31. UNHCR. *Resettlement Handbook: Division of International Protection.* United Nations. 2002.

- Survivors of violence or torture
- Those in need of medical treatment that cannot be obtained in the country of refuge
- Mentally or physically disabled refugees
- Those for whom there is no other secure solution

Groups designated under the P-2 category currently include Iranian religious minorities, Somali Bantu in Kenya, Cubans under persecution because of religious or political beliefs (among others in Cuba), religious minorities within the former Soviet Union, and qualifying Vietnamese.[32]

September 11 has prompted a reassessment of the priority system in refugee admissions. Bill Frelick, Director of the U.S. Committee for Refugees, proposes limiting the P-1 category and creating additional priorities by promoting certain current P-1 principles into separate priority categories. An example of this would be to create an independent priority category for mentally or physically disabled refugees.[33] David A. Martin, in his report to the Department of State on the U.S. Refugee Admissions Program, addressed Frelick's proposal, recommended less drastic changes to the priority system including removing the P-4 and P-5 categories (reserved for distant relatives of refugees, though no nationalities are currently designated for the P-4 or P-5 categories) as well as wider use of the P-2 category.[34]

Refugee admissions that arrive at consulates are reviewed under what is known by Visas 93. Visas 93 is available to the spouse and children of a refugee; however, the parents of refugees, which are covered under the P-3 category, are not eligible for admission to the United States under Visas 93.[35] Problems then arise because the

---

32. Kuck, Charles. Statement Before the Senate Judiciary Subcommittee on Immigration, Border Security, and Citizenship. 9 September 2004.

33. Frelick, Bill. Rethinking U.S. Refugee Admissions: Quantity and Quality, World Refugee Survey 2002, at 28, 35.

34. Martin, David A. "The United States Refugee Admissions Program: Reforms for a New Era of Refugee Resettlement." U.S. Department of State. Washington: GPO, 2004.

35. 9 Foreign Affairs Manual Appendix O. U.S. Department of State. 11 April 2002.

P-3 category is reserved only for members of certain nationalities. Furthermore, Visas 93 cases are more complex than other cases that consular officers encounter because approval for refugee status requires coordination between several departments within the U.S. government, including the International Organization for Migration (IOM).[36] The IOM loans money for the cost of transportating the refugee and performs health screening prior to departure. The Office of Refugee Resettlement (ORR) under the Department of Health and Human Services provides the necessary medical and cash assistance for refugees when they are admitted into the U.S.[37] These cases are "dauntingly labor-intensive, meaning that the consular officer may have to postpone work on several of the more familiar types of visa applications in order to process one Visas 93 case. As a result, Visas 93 applications may simply be laid aside, languishing for many months on a desk in the consulate."[38] The wait time, combined with the complications that often arise when a refugee is required to go the Consulate to be interviewed, often results in refugees opting for use of the P-3 category to bring family into the United States, rather than Visas 93 processing through the Consulate.

On top of security concerns, the need to be vigilant against fraud plays a part in slowing down the reviewing of applications. It requires extensive coordination among different agencies and organizations, and this is part of what is fueling the drive to restructure resettlement policies.

Fraud is and has been a danger within the resettlement and asylum programs within the United States and is one of the main arguments against the inclusion of §411(a)(bb)(iii)(VII) of the USA PATRIOT Act, as discussed earlier, assuming that those spouses

---

36. "Migrant Movement Processing/Assistance." International Organization for Migration. ‹http://www.iom.int/en/what/migrant_movement.shtml›. 2004.

37. Health and Human Services. "Eligibility for Refugee Resettlement Assistance and Services through the Office of Refugee Resettlement." Office of Refugee Resettlement. ‹http://www.acf.hhs.gov/programs/orr/geninfo/index.htm›. 10 November 2003.

38. Martin, David A. "The United States Refugee Admissions Program: Reforms for a New Era of Refugee Resettlement." U.S. Department of State. Washington: GPO, 2004.

and children may be sympathetic to the terrorist causes of their spouse or parent and may try to gain entry into the U.S. in an effort to infiltrate the country to carry out harmful activities.

Fear of terrorists fraudulently entering the country to attack the U.S. is a legitimate concern. Within the refugee resettlement program in a post-9/11 world, fraud largely occurs in two ways, relationship fraud, and false claims about refugee status.

With the P-3 category, reserved for family reunification, fraud often takes form through false affidavits of relationships (AOR). The P-3 category is more prone to fraud than other priority categories because the P-3 category is limited to specific nationalities designated by the attorney general. Currently, immediate family members of resettled refugees from Burma, Burundi, Congo (Brazzaville), Democratic Republic of Congo (DRC), Colombia, Cuba, Ethiopia, Eritrea, Haiti, Iran, Liberia, Rwanda, Somalia, and Sudan are eligible for P-3 resettlement,[39] though the Department of State has noted that in FY2004 individuals of sixty different nationalities were accepted as refugees.[40] While someone may claim to be related to an admitted refugee as a means to escape harm, themselves, as discussed in David Martin's report on U.S. refugee resettlement policy, others have more sinister intentions "involving buying and selling of access."[41]

Since 9/11, in an effort to reduce fraudulent applicants from being admitted to the United States, the U.S. government has created the Refugee Access Verification Unit (RAVU), a database that contains information on refugee applications. Applications for asylum and refugee status, Forms I-589 and I-590, respectively, ask specific questions about relatives such as their names, places of birth, dates of birth, and current places of residence. RAVU retains

---

39. Bureau for Population, Migration, and Refugees. "FY 2005 Report to Congress." U.S. Department of State. Washington, 2004.

40. Ereli, Adam. "Refugee Admissions for FY2004." Bureau of Population, Refugees, and Migration. Washington, 4 October 2004.

41. Martin, David A. "The United States Refugee Admissions Program: Reforms for a New Era of Refugee Resettlement." U.S. Department of State. Washington: GPO, 2004.

this information and with P-3 applications, Form I-730, the information reported on this petition is checked against the original refugee or asylum application in RAVU in an effort to reduce fraud.[42] Beginning September 11, 2001, all applications filed under the P-3 category were subject to review by the RAVU. This review caused many delays and "many refugees who thought they had been fully approved for resettlement in the United States found themselves in limbo for months and a great many for years."[43]

Though many delays were attributed to post-9/11 increased security checks, and surely increased security checks did contribute to delays, the majority of delays were due to the anti-fraud reviews. One case was documented in the *San Francisco Chronicle*. Olive Briggs, a resettled refugee originally from Sierra Leone, petitioned for her mother, sister, and adopted daughter to join her in the United States, but was required to wait years for her family to join her; during the interim, her mother died. The newspaper, perhaps incorrectly, attributed the delays to increased security checks; in any case, the story illustrates the lengthy delays that some refugees have experienced in their effort to reunite with family members. Delays in refugee cases are of particular concern because, if there is no evidence of fraud, the refugee may be waiting in an area that is not safe. As discussed in the article, "We know people who have been murdered, who have died of diseases, who have been raped, deported or incarcerated. There are serious consequences when people are kept in this limbo."[44]

---

42. Federal Register. "Privacy Act of 1974; System of Records." 26 December 2002.

43. Martin, David A. "The United States Refugee Admissions Program: Reforms for a New Era of Refugee Resettlement." U.S. Department of State. Washington: GPO, 2004.

44. Hendrix, Anastasia. "Post-9/11 Delays Hurt US-Bound Refugees." San Francisco Chronicle. 30 November 2003.

FORMS USED IN REFUGEE/ASYLUM PROCESSING

I-589 — U.S. immigration form used to apply for asylum status

I-590 — U.S. immigration form used to apply for refugee status

I-730 — U.S. immigration form to petition for an alien relative of refugees or asylees

AOR — Affidavit of Relationship; used to declare the relationship of a family member

In addition to relationship fraud, fraud can also take the form of false claims about refugee status in general. Resettlement in the United States is highly desirable. As one expert on refugees explained, "resettlement usually represents major gains in life prospects, often well beyond even what the nondisplaced local population living near the refugees could ever reasonably expect. Hence the temptation is great."[45] This type of fraud is particularly unnerving because, if the "refugee" is successful, it represents the possibility of someone entering the U.S., often from very dangerous areas of the world, by dubious means. And while one hopes that such an instance of fraud was only an effort to increase life opportunities and wealth, it can signal that someone was entering the United States for less acceptable reasons.

Fraud is often the focus of asylum applications, particularly since two convicted in the 1993 WTC bombing, Sheik Omar Abdel Rahman[46] and Ramzi Yousef,[47] had fraudulently asked for asylum. Since terrorism within the United States has become a reality, asylum has been an issue of competing viewpoints. The government simultaneously embraces and rejects it.

---

45. Martin, David A. "The United States Refugee Admissions Program: Reforms for a New Era of Refugee Resettlement." U.S. Department of State. Washington: GPO, 2004.
46. Clines, Francis X. "The Twin Towers: After Bombing, New Scrutiny for Holes in Immigration Net." New York Times. 11 March 1993: A1.
47. "World Trade Center Bombing Trial Goes to Jury." CNN News. ⟨http://www.cnn.com/US/9711/05/trade.center.trial/index.html⟩. 5 November 1997.

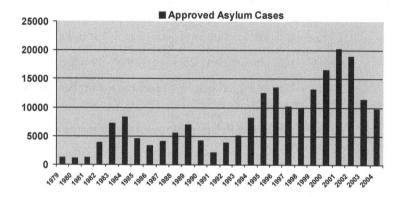

This dichotomy is evident in the manner in which asylees are handled in the country. In FY2003, the U.S. granted asylum to 11,434 individuals;[48] however, Congress has imposed a cap of 10,000 on the number of asylees that are allowed to adjust their status to that of legal permanent resident (LPR). Since 1995 there has been a significant backlog in the number of asylees waiting to adjust their status; without intervention from Congress, many of these asylees will have to wait ten to fifteen years before they can become legal permanent residents and an additional five years after that to become citizens of the U.S. Scott Busby, PRM's Director of Policy and Resource Planning, expressed what a hindrance this cap creates for asylees. He said that essentially, his office's hands were tied in trying to remedy the situation. An act of Congress would be required to increase the number of asylees allowed to adjust their status.[49]

The cap was originally introduced in the Refugee Act of 1980. The cap allotted for asylum adjustments was set at 5,000, a number that was quickly reached.[50] In 1983, 7,215 persons were granted

---

48. "FY 2003 Yearbook of Immigration Statistics." U.S. Citizenship and Immigration Services. ⟨http://uscis.gov/graphics/shared/aboutus/statistics/IMM03yrbk/IMM2003list.htm⟩. 24 September 2004.

49. Busby, Scott. Personal interview with author. 29 June 2004.

50. 8 U.S.C. 1159(b). P.L. 96-212. "Refugee Act of 1980." United States. 17 March 1980.

asylum.[51] In an effort to clear up the backlog, in 1990 under the Immigration Act the cap was doubled to 10,000.[52] This measure was beneficial until, in 1995, the number of people granted asylum grew beyond the cap, thus creating a backlog again, one that has ballooned to tens of thousands of people.[53]

Particularly in the aftermath of 9/11, it would not be a politically popular move to raise the cap of asylee adjustments; however, it is irresponsible for the United States to continue in its current cycle of approving upwards of 20,000 asylum cases a year while not allowing them to adjust their status. It serves no purpose to proceed in such a way. Not adjusting the status of those granted asylum does not increase the security of the United States.

It is important here to recognize that this issue has serious consequences. Essentially, if one is granted asylum but must wait a decade or more to become a LPR, the benefits one can receive while in the United States are limited. With LPR status, certain rights and protections are afforded; however, without that status asylees are in a state of limbo. They are in the United States legally and permanently but they are not offered the same protections and benefits as others in similar circumstances.

In December 2002, the United States and Canada signed an agreement known at the "Safe Third Country Agreement" which states that those seeking asylum at a land point of entry (POE) cannot cross the border from Canada to the U.S. or vice versa to seek asylum; an asylum claim must be made in the country in which one is present.[54] This agreement, as explained by Canadian Deputy Prime Minister John Manley, was created in an effort to improve security and eradicate "the practice of asylum shopping by refugee applicants, by allowing their return to the last safe country from

---

51. "FY 2003 Yearbook of Immigration Statistics." U.S. Citizenship and Immigration Services. 2004.

52. P.L. 101-649 §104(a)(1).

53. Ewing, Walter. "Lives in Limbo: Mismanagement of a Bad Policy Leave Asylees in No Man's Land." The American Immigration Law Foundation. August 2003.

54. United States. "Safe Third Country Agreement." December 2002.

which they came."[55] The concept of "asylum shopping" is founded on the assumption that asylum might be denied on the basis of failure to prove refugee status as defined by the Refugee Convention of 1951.

Directly related to the attacks of September 11, this agreement is a component of a "30-point action plan" as outlined in the Smart Border Declaration signed by both DHS Secretary Tom Ridge and Canadian Deputy Prime Minister John Manley in December 2001.[56] Point four of this agreement states, "Review refugee/asylum practices and procedures to ensure that applicants are thoroughly screened for security risks and take necessary steps to share information on refugee and asylum claimants."[57] The inclusion of this point raises two concerns. First, it questions the security procedures that were used by both the Canadian and American governments in regard to screening asylum applicants prior to 9/11 as well as the information sharing between the two governments on asylum cases. Second, it presumes that asylum applicants pose a security threat until proven otherwise and that claims should be assumed fraudulent until refugee status can be justified. It is understandable that proper security clearance procedures should be followed, particularly since examples of terrorists seeking asylum in the U.S. for suspicious purposes can be found in the 1993 WTC bombing case. And while fraud is a justifiable concern in all immigration claims, many people have valid claims for asylum.

AILA Canada outlines six flaws within the Safe Third Country Agreement. Though this agreement exempts those seeking family reunification in the Canada or the U.S., as AILA Canada discusses, it does not include *de facto* family members. The point is also made that while both the U.S.'s and Canada' immigration laws pertaining to refugees and asylees are guided by the 1951 Convention, the two

---

55. "'Safe Third Country' Pact Puts Refugees." CBC News Canada. 17 December 2002.

56. "United States and Canada to Implement Safe Third Country Agreement on Asylum." U.S. Department of Homeland Security. 8 March 2004.

57. Smart Border Declaration. 12 December 2001.

countries have interpreted the guidelines of the Convention differently, which can have implications for asylum seekers. Other points made by AILA Canada discuss the ambiguity and lack of guidance the Agreement provides to the detriment of the asylum seeker. Perhaps one of the strongest arguments against the Safe Third Country Agreement is the U.S.'s practice of detaining some of those seeking asylum in the United States. [58]

Asylum in the United States is granted through one of two processes. In affirmative processing, the individual requests asylum within one year of arriving in the United States. Within forty-three days of filing the application for asylum, the individual is scheduled for an interview with an asylum officer to determine if that person meets the definition of a refugee and is not subject to any bars to refugee status (i.e. persecuted others, engaged in terrorist activity, etc.). Within sixty days, a decision should be made regarding the case. Though the USCIS sets target dates of forty-three days from the time of filing to the time of an interview and sixty days from the time of the interview to the time of adjudication, these timeframes seem to be unrealistic. The Department of Homeland Security releases a monthly report of immigration statistics in which the August 2004 report stated that there were 197,066 asylum cases pending,[59] making it highly unlikely that target timeframes will be met.

What is more troubling and what may make Canada a more desirable option is the way in which some asylees, coming to the shores of the United States for refuge, are treated. Under Operation Liberty Shield, implemented on March 17, 2003, people from thirty-three countries are to be automatically detained when entering the United States to seek asylum. This does not pertain to those who are already in the U.S. legally under a different status and who file form

58. "AILA's Canada Chapter Comments on Safe Third Country Regulations." AILA Canada. ⟨http://www.aila.org/contentViewer.aspx?bc=9,576,2199,2205⟩. 26 December 2002.

59. Office of Immigration Statistics. "Immigration Monthly Statistical Report." U.S. Department of Homeland Security. Washington, 30 September 2004.

I-589, Application for Asylum. As DHS Secretary Tom Ridge explained,[60]

> The detention of asylum seekers is basically predicated on one basic notion. We just want to make sure that those who are seeking asylum, number one, are who they say they are and, two, are legitimately seeking refuge in our country because of political repression at home, not because they choose to cause harm or bring destruction to our shores.

A press statement released by the U.S. Department of Homeland Security stated, in regard to new asylum procedures:[61]

> Asylum applicants from nations where al-Qaeda, al-Qaeda sympathizers, and other terrorist groups are known to have operated will be detained for the duration of their processing period. This reasonable and prudent temporary action allows authorities to maintain contact with asylum seekers while we determine the validity of their claim. DHS and the Department of State will coordinate exceptions to this policy.

While detentions are for those from "nations where al-Qaeda, al-Qaeda sympathizers, and other terrorist groups are know to have operated," this statement brings up again the argument as to whether this is protecting the United States. It is the same criticism that NSEERS faced. Though thirty-three countries are believed to be the target of Operation Liberty Shield (the countries were not made public, however, they are believed to include Iraq, Afghanistan, Algeria, Bahrain, Bangladesh, Djibouti, Egypt, Eritrea, Indonesia, Iran, Jordan, Kazakhstan, Kuwait, Lebanon, Libya, Malaysia, Morocco, Oman, Pakistan, Philippines, Qatar, Saudi Arabia, Somalia, Sudan, Syria, Thailand, Tajikistan, Tunisia, Turkey, Turkmenistan, United Arab Emirates, Uzbekistan, and Yemen[62]) it has been proven time and again, as the terrorist attack in Spain in

---

60. Ridge, Tom. Press Conference. 18 March 2003.

61. "Operation Liberty Shield." U.S. Department of Homeland Security. 17 March 2003.

62. "Assessing the New Normal: Liberty and Security for the Post-September 11 United States." Lawyers Committee for Human Rights. September 2003.

2004 illustrates, that terrorists are not limited to thirty-three countries. To detain an individual for weeks while waiting to adjudicate an asylum claim seriously calls into question the civil liberties of that person in exchange for what may or may not be added protection to the United States is a deeply flawed system that creates the façade of security. There is a fine line between implementing policy to prevent terrorism and treating individuals with basic rights. Perhaps it would be beneficial for the United States to develop practices and policies that are fair, yet work to fully protect the country by treating all who come to our shores equally.

It may be more important than ever, in a post-9/11 world, to resettle refugees. As discussed by immigration attorney and AILA treasurer Charles Kuck, the United States has a moral and international commitment to resettle refugees. At a hearing before the Senate Subcommittee on Immigration, Border Security, and Citizenship, he stated, "A well-run refugee program is an important component in our security arsenal because it helps to ameliorate situations that are ripe for exploitation by our nation's foes. At the same time, a well-run program also will help to fulfill our moral and international obligations, thereby enhancing our nation's reputation in the international community."[63]

---

63. *Ibid.*

6. The Future of Immigration Policy

All Americans, with the exception of Native Americans, have some connection to immigration as either immigrants themselves or as descendents of immigrants. It is important that immigration policy be created and implemented in a way that recognizes and embraces the benefits of immigration on which this country was built. At the same time, the requirement of balancing this welcoming spirit with the need to protect the country from terrorism cannot be overlooked.

This balance is largely the responsibility of the Department of Homeland Security and three agencies within the Department: the Citizenship and Immigration Services, Customs and Border Protection, and Investigations and Customs Enforcement. Since the duties and responsibilities of the Immigration and Naturalization Service were divided among these agencies, it remains to be seen how well these agencies work together. Though intra-agency communication was not the forte of the INS, dividing the agency into three and placing them under the Department of Homeland Security has created a structure that requires communication across agencies. The future of immigration in the United States largely depends on how well these agencies interact with each other, the people they serve, and other agencies within the U.S. government.

Changes in immigration laws may be implemented. However, without strong leadership and oversight it is unlikely that positive change will be made. The creation of an ombudsman for the USCIS was a start, but we have yet to see how effective this office will be and whether it will positively impact immigration operations in the United States. It is also interesting that immigration now comes under the Department of Homeland Security, an area of government that deals exclusively with protecting the United States and its people from future attacks; the inclusion of legacy INS agencies into this department is an indicator of the perspective in which the American government views immigrants.

One of the biggest problems that the agencies governing immigration in the U.S. must overcome is the need to communicate across agencies. Information sharing may be one of the strongest tools in facilitating the distribution of benefits to immigrants and to preventing terrorism. Several laws have been put into place that mandate information sharing, such as provisions in the Enhanced Border Security and Visa Reform Act of 2003, requiring the Department of State to share visa issuance information with border officers and USCIS officials.[1] Provisions regarding information sharing have also been included in laws such as the USA PATRIOT Act, the Intelligence Authorization Act of 2004, the Intelligence Authorization Act of 2005, and the Homeland Security Act. The 9/11 Commission also echoed the need for increased sharing of information across agencies. This was also the subject of a Senate subcommittee hearing on September 23, 2003, entitled, "Information Sharing and Coordination for Visa Issuance: Our First Line of Defense for Homeland Security."[2] And while it is still fairly early to determine whether the level of communication between the agencies that govern immigration has improved, change is often slow.

1. P.L. 107-173. Enhanced Border Security and Visa Entry Reform Act of 2002. 14 May 2002.

2. U.S. Senate. "Information Sharing and Coordination for Visa Issuance: Our First Line of Defense for Homeland Security." Immigration and Border Security Subcommittee Hearing. 23 September 2003.

Notably, in terms of international students, the SEVIS database that was implemented after 9/11 has been the source of frustrations caused by a lack of communication. Only after an article appeared in *The Chronicle of Higher Education* did Immigration and Custom Enforcement officials share information regarding students who had been terminated in SEVIS with border officials.[3]

Furthermore, students are in a unique predicament in that the database used to track all international students studying in the U.S. is managed and monitored by Immigration and Customs Enforcement, while all adjudications are completed under the U.S. Citizenship and Immigration Services. Frequently, school officials report, there is a lack of communication between the two agencies resulting is extensive waiting periods, errors in the SEVIS database, and matters that take months if not years to resolve. One school official reports having to wait for more than a year for an answer to a reinstatement of status case because of a lack of communication and efficiency between USCIS and ICE. The case was denied, but after the USCIS adjudicated the denial, it becomes the responsibility of the ICE to process and monitor the removal of that student.[4]

Cross-communication is often hindered because of the politics involved with immigration work. Immigration policy has long been a political pawn in the United States and will continue to be, to the further detriment of immigrants and the American people as a whole. Under the George W. Bush administration, immigration policy was the subject of a series of contradictory actions. In January 2004, President Bush proposed offering three-year work visas to illegal immigrants residing in the United States, yet H-1B temporary work visas and H-2B visas for legal immigrants were exhausted by February and March, respectively, of that same year.[5] Former Secretary of State Colin Powell was quoted as saying, "We want to preserve and even expand the benefits of openness"[6]; yet, the U.S.

---

3. NAFSA. "SEVIS Conference Call: Policy Issues." NAFSA: Association of International Educators. <www.nafsa.org/content/ProfessionalandEducationalResources/ ImmigrationAdvisingResources/nglu2004e.pdf>. 12 May 2004.

4. Anonymous. Personal Interview with Author. 7 May 2004.

5. Lamourie, Matthew. "Will Election Politics Kill Visa Reform?" *The Boston Globe*. 20 April 2004. A15.

government's actions towards immigrants, including implementing policies such as NSEERS, project a considerably less welcoming ideal.

Additionally, in December 2004 President Bush nominated Bernard Kerik to head the Department of Homeland Security after Secretary Tom Ridge resigned. Shortly after the President made his choice known, Kerik withdrew his name from consideration because, for one thing, he had hired a nanny who may not have been in legal immigration status.[7] This is problematic; as Secretary of the Department of Homeland Security, Kerik would have been responsible for overseeing the immigration agencies of the U.S. However, it is not clear whether the Bush administration knew about Kerik's problems prior to asking him to head the Department of Homeland Security or if they would have continued to support him had he not withdrawn from consideration for the job. The new Secretary of Homeland Security must make a concerted effort to balance the desire to welcome legitimate immigrants and to keep the U.S. secure. Currently, the policies have leaned towards the more restrictive.

There remains the question of how increasingly restrictive U.S. immigration policies may affect citizens of the United States. Under the rules of reciprocity in immigration law throughout the world, policies that the United States has implemented on foreign nationals will be applied to Americans traveling outside the U.S., as well. Citizens of the United States now have machine-readable passports, as the U.S. requires of those entering this country. Also, since the implementation of US-VISIT, requiring the photographing and fingerprinting of foreign nationals coming to the U.S., Brazil has implemented a similar procedure for Americans visiting the country. Should the Visa Waiver Program be eliminated in the U.S., it is almost certain that United States citizens will be required to obtain visas for entry into most Western European countries and many of the other countries that currently participate in the program.

---

6. Powell, Colin. "Secure Borders, Open Doors." *The Washington Post.* 21 April 2004.

7. Associated Press. "Kerik Withdraws His Name for DHS Chief." ABC News. ⟨http://abcnews.go.com/Politics/wireStory?id=320415⟩. 10 December 2004.

Though these are minor examples of how immigration policy affects U.S. citizens, there is no doubt that tightened immigration policies in the United States will continue to threaten the freedoms that American citizens enjoy.

Treating immigrants unjustly under the pretext of fighting terrorism will slowly but surely erode the rights of citizens as well. The Pentagon in 2003 proposed a data-mining program called "Total Information Awareness," later renamed the "Terrorism Information Awareness" (TIA). This program sought to create technology that would allow the United States government to obtain information on individuals, both citizens and noncitizens, in regards to terrorism concerns. John Poindexter, former director of the Information Awareness Office at the Defense Advanced Research Projects Agency, stated in an op-ed piece for the *New York Times*, "Research is being conducted on technologies that will keep the identities of subjects hidden from analysts, but still allow the detection of patterns of terrorist activities."[8]

The TIA program, as explained in a May 2003 report to Congress, is largely based on analysts imagining potential terrorist attack scenarios and then using the technology of TIA to obtain information in regard to resources and means that would be utilized to carry out such attacks. As the report concedes, "There will always be uncertainty and ambiguity in interpreting the information available. Thus, different hypotheses would be developed by the analysts to reflect their differing points of view."[9] While Congress rejected the full implementation of the TIA program (the rejected components included those that pertained to the privacy issues of U.S. citizens), some provisions of the program, those pertaining to foreign nationals, remained. Congress required approval before TIA would be used with U.S. citizens suspected of terrorist ties; however, foreign nationals do not receive the same protections.

It is understandable that noncitizens would not enjoy the same freedoms and protections as citizens; however, the TIA program is

---

8. Poindexter, John M. "Finding the Face of Terror in Data." *The New York Times*. 10 September 2003.
9. Ibid.

worrisome on many levels. First and foremost, this program was originally designed to be used on citizens, allowing the government to obtain information without permission from the individual and without prior approval from courts or appropriate government agencies. Secondly, it is highly conceivable that, should another terrorist attack occur within United States borders, the push to provide the government with tools to fight terrorism such as TIA would increase at the expense of citizens' privacy, freedom, and civil liberties.

The TIA, a program that negatively affects noncitizens, is not the only example of a policy that has the potential to also negatively affect Americans. Perhaps some of the most troublesome measures that were discussed in Congress were included in the Domestic Security Enhancement Act of 2003, also known as the Patriot Act II. A summary of the draft legislation was obtained in early 2003 by the Center for Public Integrity from the Department of Justice. It included provisions that revoked the citizenship of Americans accused of terrorism. Section 311 of this draft allowed for the sharing of information on foreign nationals and U.S. citizens between the U.S. government and other countries. The summary states:[10]

> Section 203 and other provisions of the USA PATRIOT Act broadened authority to share information among federal agencies that may be relevant to the detection and prevention of terrorism, and to obtain otherwise confidential information for use in terrorism investigations. That Act, however, did not adequately address the need for enhanced information sharing authority in relation to state and local officials and foreign governments, who are the critical partners of the United States in investigating terrorist crimes and preventing future terrorist attacks. This section of the bill would provide further authority for sharing of consumer credit information, visa-related information, and educational records information with state and local law enforcement, thereby enacting the remainder of the information sharing proposals that have been proposed legislatively and endorsed by the Administration and the Department of Justice.

10. U.S. Department of Justice. Draft Summary of Domestic Security Enhancement Act of 2003. 9 January 2003.

The Patriot Act II, however, was greatly reduced in scope by the time parts were signed into law by President Bush under the Intelligence Authorization Act for Fiscal Year 2004 on December 13, 2003, largely because of the public outcry after reading the draft. This revised bill, however, when signed by the President, did contain a provision similar to the draft summary regarding the release of financial information.

Section 374 of the law states:

SEC. 374. MODIFICATION TO DEFINITION OF FINANCIAL INSTITUTION IN RIGHT TO FINANCIAL PRIVACY ACT.

(a) MODIFICATION OF DEFINITION. — Section 1114 of the Right to Financial Privacy Act of 1978 (12 U.S.C. 3414) is amended by adding at the end the following:

> (d) For purposes of this section, and sections 1115 and 1117 insofar as they relate to the operation of this section, the term "financial institution" has the same meaning as in subsections (a)(2) and (c)(1) of section 5312 of title 31, United States Code, except that, for purposes of this section, such term shall include only such a financial institution any part of which is located inside any State or territory of the United States, the District of Columbia, Puerto Rico, Guam, American Samoa, the Commonwealth of the Northern Mariana Islands, or the United States Virgin Islands."
>
> (b) CROSS REFERENCE MODIFICATION. — Section 1101(1) of such Act (12 U.S.C. 401(1)) is amended by inserting ", except as provided in section 1114," before "means any office."

In an article that appeared in *The Nation* on March 17, 2003,[11] David Cole discussed the potential for an elimination of "the

---

11. Cole, David. "Patriot Act's Big Brother." *The Nation*. 17 March 2003.

distinction between domestic terrorism and international terrorism for a host of investigatory purposes." Currently, regulations regarding the investigation of noncitizens are looser than those of citizens. Should the government prevail in broadening the intelligence gathering capabilities of investigating government agencies, this will apply the limited rights that foreign nationals experience to U.S. citizens as well.

This topic has already been the subject of debate in terms of U.S. citizens who have been linked to the al-Qaeda terrorist network and others with terrorist connections. John Walker, the so-called "American Taliban," was one of the first examples that became known to the public since terrorism came to the forefront of the national agenda. In a recent case before the Supreme Court, Jose Padilla, also known as Abdullah al Muhajir, was declared an "enemy combatant" of the United States and was militarily detained.[12] Though the Supreme Court has yet to make a final decision on this case, it raises three important points. The first is whether the U.S. can and should revoke the citizenship of someone declared to be an "enemy combatant." Second, if someone's citizenship is revoked and that person is then removed from the United States, where is that person to go? Also, what role does the Constitution play if the government has the power to declare someone a noncitizen and effectively render his protections under the Constitution moot?

Decisions on these questions can have implications for immigrants and other noncitizens as well. Anytime we throw into question the rights of noncitizens, even during an era of terrorism fear, it can have long-term consequences for citizens and noncitizens alike; this is something that should be carefully considered.

The United States is currently in a potentially dangerous position; it has been forced to reassess many policies touching on both citizens and noncitizens. Many of the policies being used to

---

12. Donald H. Rumsfeld, Secretary of Defense, Petitioner v. Jose Padilla and Donna R. Newman, as next friend of Jose Padilla.

combat terrorism by tracking foreign nationals in the U.S., and limiting their rights, have the strong possibility of blurring the line between the rights (or lack of rights) of citizens and those of noncitizens. If the situatoin is not handled correctly, the potential for limiting the civil liberties of citizens is real. The threat of reduced rights for citizens is imminent, so long as the United States continues down the slippery slope of limiting the rights of others in the name of national security. This was discussed in an article written for the *Harvard Journal of Law and Technology*. The author, Richard Sobel, makes a valid point that:[13]

> In a free society under a constitution of enumerated and delegated powers, a regime develops based upon and generating basic, retained rights for individuals as persons. This system derives from the overarching principle of governance by consent. This dimension creates a buffer around individuals and against state action. Individuals inherently possess rights and political identities.
>
> However, under a national identification system, rights are derived from credentials. People obtain ersatz-identities based on identification documents and numbers or places in databanks. The requirement to prove identity or appear in a national databank in order to obtain and exercise certain rights demeans the foundation on which free governance is based. The use of personal information for governmental action without consent or due process violates liberty and property rights.

While questions remain regarding the rights of noncitizens and citizens, illegal immigrants are on the other end of the spectrum. A discussion on the intersection of terrorism and immigration law would not be complete without an examination of illegal immigration in the United States. Post 9/11 the INS took a hard line on illegal immigration, rounding up and deporting many, though most were of Middle Eastern descent.

---

13. Sobel, Richard. "The Demeaning of Identity and Personhood in National Identification Systems." *Harvard Journal of Law and Technology*. 15(2). Spring 2002.

The vast majority of undocumented immigrants in the United States are not Arab or Muslim and therefore they garner less attention in relation to terrorism concerns. The United States has less stringent security controls for those originating fromcertain countries, but the country has recently implemented immigration laws directing additional scrutiny on others. Take the case of the detentions of many illegal individuals originally from the Middle Eastern area. These policies have a detrimental effect on the country and do little to prevent terrorism.

A report released in 2003 by the USCIS estimates that there are approximately 7 million undocumented aliens in the United States. This number grew by approximately 350,000 per year throughout the 1990s. The majority of these illegal immigrants come from Mexico, El Salvador, Colombia, Guatemala, Honduras, China, and Ecuador, with each country having more than 100,000 undocumented aliens in the U.S. Mexico has more than 4.8 million.[14] While many of these undocumented aliens are useful in performing a significant amount of unskilled labor in this country, immigration policy intended to protect the United States from threats would be incomplete if it did not address illegal immigration concerns.

Bills such as AgJobs, a bipartisan bill sponsored by Sen. Larry Craig (R-Idaho) and Sen. Edward Kennedy (D-MA), would allow illegal immigrants working as agricultural workers to gain legal permanent residency in the United States if they can show that they worked 2,060 hours or 360 work days in an agricultural occupation between September 1, 2003 and August 31, 2009.[15] The bill states in part:

---

14. USCIS. "Executive Summary: Estimates of the Unauthorized Immigration Population Residing in the United States: 1990-2000." Washington: GPO, 31 January 2003.

15. S. 1645 and H.R. 3142. Agricultural Job Opportunity, Benefits, and Security Act of 2003.

SEC. 101. AGRICULTURAL WORKERS.

(c) ADJUSTMENT TO PERMANENT RESIDENCE

(1) AGRICULTURAL WORKERS

(A) IN GENERAL — Except as provided in subparagraph (B), the Secretary shall adjust the status of an alien granted lawful temporary resident status under subsection (a) to that of an alien lawfully admitted for permanent residence if the Secretary determines that the following requirements are satisfied:

(i) QUALIFYING EMPLOYMENT — The alien has performed at least 2,060 hours or 360 work days, whichever is less, of agricultural employment in the United States, during the period beginning on September 1, 2003, and ending on August 31, 2009.

(ii) QUALIFYING YEARS — The alien has performed at least 430 hours or 75 work days, whichever is less, of agricultural employment in the United States in at least 3 nonoverlapping periods of 12 consecutive months during the period beginning on September 1, 2003, and ending on August 31, 2009. Qualifying periods under this clause may include nonconsecutive 12-month periods.

iii) QUALIFYING WORK IN FIRST 3 YEARS — The alien has performed at least 1,380 hours or 240 work days, whichever is less, of agricultural employment during the period beginning on September 1, 2003, and ending on August 31, 2006.

(iv) APPLICATION PERIOD — The alien applies for adjustment of status not later than August 31, 2010.

(v) PROOF — In meeting the requirements of clauses (i), (ii), and (iii), an alien may submit the record of employment described in subsection (a)(5) or such documentation as may be submitted under subsection (d)(3).

(vi) DISABILITY — In determining whether an alien has met the requirements of clauses (i), (ii), and (iii), the Secretary shall credit the alien with any work days lost because the alien was unable to work in agricultural employment due to injury or disease arising out of and in the course of the alien's agricultural employment, if the alien can establish such disabling injury or disease through medical records.

This bill has created controversy based on several factors. First is whether or not illegal immigrants should be essentially rewarded for being in the United States illegally. As the conservative publication *Human Events* points out, "Lawbreakers would get an initial reward for their lawbreaking, a legal work permit and legal permission to stay here. Later they receive permanent U.S. residency. They even gain the right to become U.S. citizens!"[16]

This debate also expands to a larger discussion about illegal immigrant workers in the U.S. in general. It is often asserted that the U.S. needs low-skilled foreign laborers because they are willing to do jobs that Americans are not. The flip side of that discussion is that American workers are willing to do jobs currently filled by unskilled illegal laborers; however, illegal immigrants are willing to work for much less money and Americans are not willing to do these jobs for wages below the minimum living wage.

The final point in the debate surrounding AgJobs is the potential for fraud. Since these workers are residing and working in the country illegally, it may prove difficult to establish documented evidence of the length of time they have spent in the U.S., the type of job held, and number of hours worked. The fear of fraud is further exacerbated by the fact that Mahmud Abouhalima, one of the perpetrators in the 1993 WTC bombing, exploited a similar provision in the Immigration Reform and Control Act of 1986.[17]

Much of immigration policy in the United States is reactionary. Change often comes about after a weakness in the system is determined to exist. In the plethora of laws that affected immigration after the terrorist attacks of 1993 and 2001, it is

---

16. Edwards, James R. Jr. Republicans Rewarding Illegal Aliens. *Human Events*. 1 October 2004.

17. Camarota, Steven. Remarks at Cato Institute's Policy Forum. 16 January 2004.

imperative that the United States government carefully assesses the needs of the country, its citizens, and the noncitizens residing here or planning to visit the country. In the whirlwind of terrorism concerns, it is easy to overlook the fundamental role that immigration plays within this country. Nonimmigrants visiting the United States contribute millions of dollars to the country each year. In addition, the cross-cultural experience that many visitors have in the United States helps to build understanding and positive relationships between the United States and other countries.

Former Secretary of State Colin Powell has proposed an "open doors, secure borders" policy for the government to consider when creating immigration laws. This is an ideal concept for the United States to adopt; however, thus far the country has done a poor job of adhering to that focus. It is a difficult task to balance the benefits and risks. Factors to weigh include the positive economic impact of foreign tourists, the need to maintain positive immigration relations with ally countries, the need to consider the reciprocal consequences of immigration laws on U.S. citizens traveling abroad, and security concerns.

Current immigration policies are largely flawed to the detriment of those noncitizens coming to the United States and to the country as a whole. It is important to create policies that enable those who are entitled to come to the country to do so, while deterring those who may pose a threat to the U.S.

U.S. immigration laws address security concerns in a reactionary way, based on past attacks. The history of U.S. immigration laws illustrate the history of the United States, from policies towards the Japanese in World War II to the registration of Iranians during the Iran hostage crisis, and most recently NSEERS and SEVIS. There have always been threats to U.S. security and there will continue to be threats. To maintain the integrity of U.S. immigration law and security, immigration policies that address security in a preventative and proactive manner must be instituted.

The immigration and security systems of the United States may have been overhauled in the past decade, but problems still persist. In November 2004, two Moroccan men on a U.S. no-fly list boarded an Air France flight headed towards Dulles Airport near Washington, DC.[18] The men, Abdeluala Lahiti and Mohammed Oukassou, were allowed on the flight even though airlines transporting passengers from foreign countries are required to prescreen passengers to ensure that their immigration documents are valid and, presumably, to determine if they are eligible to fly into the United States. The incident in November 2004 was the second in just a few months in which someone listed on the "no-fly" list was allowed to board an international flight to the United States. In September 2004, Cat Stevens, a.k.a. Yusuf Islam, was detained and later deported for unspecified security concerns. A spokesperson for the U.S. Department of Homeland Security stated, "The intelligence community has come into possession of additional information that raises concerns about him."[19] He was similarly removed from Israel during the 1980s for supporting Islamic extremists.[20] Under the Illegal Immigration Reform and Immigrant Responsibility Act of 1996, airlines that fail to prescreen passengers to assist in determining their eligibility to fly into the United States may be subject to fines or could be prohibited from flying into the U.S.[21]

Part of the overhaul that the U.S. has implemented in the wake of 9/11 is the passage of the Intelligence Bill in December 2004. Much of the difficulty in getting the bill passed was due to opposition led by House Judiciary Committee Chairman James Sensenbrenner (R-WI), who raised concerns regarding immigration provisions that were omitted from the bill. Sensenbrenner unsuccessfully urged Congress to include provisions that would prohibit illegal immigrants from being granted drivers' licenses and that would

---

18. "Air France Flight to Diverted, Two Passengers Detained." *Boston Globe Online.* ⟨http://www.boston.com/news/local/massachusetts/articles/2004/11/21/air⟩. 21 November 2004.

19. "Cat Stevens 'shock' at U.S. Refusal." BBC News. ⟨http://news.bbc.co.uk/2/hi/uk_news/ 3682434.stm⟩. 23 September 2004.

20. Ibid.

21. P.L. 104-208. Illegal Immigration Reform and Immigrant Responsibility Act. 30 September 1996.

limit the appeals process for foreign nationals facing deportation from the United States.[22] The bill that was signed into law by President Bush on December 17, 2004, however, did contain several immigration provisions.

Title V of the Act addresses border protection, immigration, and visa matters.[23] This includes the creation of a pilot program that will:[24]

(1) Use of advanced technological systems, including sensors, video, and unmanned aerial vehicles, for border surveillance.

(2) Use of advanced computing and decision integration software for —

(A) evaluation of data indicating border incursions;

(B) assessment of threat potential; and

(C) rapid real-time communication, monitoring, intelligence gathering, deployment, and response.

(3) Testing of advanced technology systems and software to determine best and most cost-effective uses of advanced technology to improve border security.

(4) Operation of the program in remote stretches of border lands with long distances between 24-hour ports of entry with a relatively small presence of United States border patrol officers.

(5) Capability to expand the program upon a determination by the Secretary that expansion would be an appropriate and cost-effective means of improving border security.

Subsequent sections of the Act require the Secretary of Homeland Security to create reports and recommendations regarding border security as well as increase the number of border patrol agents and immigration and customs enforcement

---

22. Henry, Ed and Ted Barrett. "House Approves Intelligence Bill." CNN News. ⟨http://www.cnn.com/2004/ALLPOLITICS/12/07/intelligence.bill⟩. 7 December 2004.

23. P.L. 108-458. Intelligence Reform and Terrorism Prevention Act of 2004. 17 December 2004.

24. P.L. 108-458 §5102(a). Intelligence Reform and Terrorism Prevention Act of 2004. 17 December 2004.

investigators. In typical government fashion, this Act mandates steps that will be necessary to recognize weaknesses within the immigration system; however, it does not establish a clear plan as to how these reports and recommendations will be utilized to create change and improvement. Furthermore, the Act does not clearly define how funding will be established for the mandated pilot programs, the research needed to compile reports and recommendations, and the hiring of new immigration officials.

Though the Intelligence Bill seeks to improve national security partly through more immigration controls, other ways to improve security should also be explored. Hatred and extremism are invigorated by ignorance. One of the most effective ways to combat this ignorance is to foster understanding through cultural exchanges. The current policies of the U.S. do not promote understanding of its culture or others. This is not a new concept and was utilized during the Cold War in a program coordinated by the CIA and the State Department.[25] In an article in *Foreign Affairs* magazine, Helena K. Finn makes the point that:[26]

> If the United States wants to cultivate a better image of itself overseas, it should concentrate on five areas of activity in particular: encouraging foreign educational reforms; extending existing foreign exchange programs; improving the access of foreign publics to American institutions and values; encouraging better cross-cultural understanding at home; and revitalizing American volunteerism abroad.

While an increase in understanding may not have immediate results, the future of the United States largely depends on how it is perceived and received throughout this increasingly global world. Now more than ever, it is necessary to increase cultural exchanges rather than shutting the country off from the rest of the world. It is important to recognize that the majority of those coming to the

---

25. Finn, Helena K. "The Case for Cultural Diplomacy." *Foreign Affairs.* 82(6). November/December 2003.
    26. *Ibid.*

United States have no intentions of harming the country or its people.

The future of immigration law in the United States has never been less certain than it is today. The United States has yet to strike a balance between security and immigration. This being said, a country whose main focus is security has allowed gaping loopholes to remain in its immigration system. There must be a determined effort to close these loopholes while allowing those who are eligible to come to the United States legally to do so without undue hindrance.

INDEX

9/11 Commission, 11, 32, 64, 69, 71, 160

A
Abid, Mohammed, 11
Abouhalima, Mahmud, 5, 13, 14, 16, 17, 18, 170
Agricultural Workers, 14
Ahmed, Nasser, 28
AILA Canada, 154
Ajaj, Mohammad Ahmad, 9, 11, 66
Alghamdi, Ahmed, 97, 105
Al-Qaeda, 77
Al-Shehhi, Marwan, 57, 59, 62, 69, 70, 97, 105, 111
American Association of Collegiate Registrars and Admissions Officers (AACRAO), 105, 121
American Civil Liberties Union (ACLU), 79, 92
American Immigration Lawyers Association (AILA), 78, 154, 157
American-Arab Anti-Discrimination Committee, 40, 80
Anti-Terrorism and Effective Death Penalty Act of 1996, 4
Anti-Terrorism and Effective Death Penalty Act of 1996 (AEDPA), 4, 22, 27, 29, 30, 41
Ashcroft, John, 48, 53, 76, 77, 79, 90
Asylum, 82, 131, 151, 155, 156
Asylum and Fraud, 148, 151
Atta, Mohamed, 32, 57, 59, 62, 63, 69, 70, 97, 105, 111
Ayyad, Nidal, 18, 19

B

Bangladesh, 73, 79, 156
Bin Laden, Osama, 10
Border Security, 60, 85, 86, 157, 160
Bureau of Population, Refugees, and Migration, 132, 134, 136

C

Canada, 77, 78, 84, 153, 154, 155
Central Index System (CIS-INS), 64, 66
Citizenship, 50, 53, 83, 135, 157, 159, 161
Computer-Assisted Passenger Pre-screening System (CAPPS), 32
Consular Affairs, 60, 84, 86
Consular Consolidated Database (CCD), 64, 65
Consular Lookout and Support System (CLASS), 64, 65
Coordinated Interagency Partnership Regulating International Students (CIPRIS), 47, 102, 103, 104, 109
Crowe Commission, 2
Customs and Border Protection (CBP), 50, 53, 63, 159

D

Demore v. Kim, 39
Department of Homeland Security (DHS), 41, 42, 47, 48, 50, 51, 65, 67, 68, 74, 76, 83, 91, 92, 128, 135, 137, 145, 146, 154, 155, 156, 159, 160, 162, 172
Dr. Germ, 90
Due Process, 39

E

Ekstrand, Laurie, 54, 57
Enhanced Border Security and Visa Entry Reform Act, 85, 91, 106

F

Federal Bureau of Investigations (FBI), 5,
8, 46, 63, 83, 90
Foreign Affairs Manual, 69
Foreign Terrorist Organizations, 4, 23, 27
Freedom of Information Act, 79, 84

G

General Accounting Office (GAO), 7, 37,
38, 54, 56, 57, 58, 59, 60, 61, 90
George Washington Bridge, 8
Green Card - See Permanent Residency,
4, 8, 9, 12, 13

H

Hamas, 4
Hanjour, Hani, 97, 105, 126
Harty, Maura, 60
Holland Tunnel, 8
Homeland Security Act, 49, 50, 51, 56, 160
Hussein, Saddam, 9

I

IDENT Database, 65
Illegal Immigration, 22, 30, 42, 97, 110, 111,
122, 172
Illegal Immigration Reform and Immi-
grant Responsibility Act of 1996
(IIRIRA), 30, 31, 32, 33, 34, 35, 36,
38, 39, 40, 41, 42, 46, 47, 97, 103, 104,
105, 122, 128
Immigration and Nationality Act (INA),
21, 22, 23, 31, 74, 81, 86, 139
Section 245(i), 17
Immigration and Naturalization Service
(INS), 9
Immigration Reform and Control Act of
1986 (IRCA), 14
INS v. St. Cyr, 40
Intensive English Programs (IEP), 121,
127
Interagency Border Information System
(IBIS), 63, 65
Interim Student and Exchange Authenti-
cation System (ISEAS), 103, 106,

107, 109
International Civil Aviation Organiza-
tion (ICAO), 67
International Organization for Migra-
tion (IOM), 137, 148
International Students, 97, 103, 122
Investigations and Customs Enforce-
ment (ICE), 34, 50, 53, 62, 109, 127,
145, 161
Ismoil, Eyad, 12, 13, 18, 104

J

Jarrah, Ziad Samir, 69, 70
Jewish Defense League, 4

K

Kach, 4
Kahane Chai, 4
Kahane, Rabbi Meir, 4
Kenya, 2, 32, 46, 147
KSM-See Mohammed, Khalid Shaikh

L

Lautenberg Amendment, 133

M

Martin, David A., 135, 145, 147
Meissner, Doris, 9, 61, 64, 109
Mexico, 31, 35, 71, 93, 168
Migration Policy Institute, 93
Mohammed, Khalid Shaikh (KSM), 11
Moussaoui, Habib Zacarias, 66

N

NAFSA
Association of International Educators, 78, 86, 102, 121
National Academy of Public Administration, 54
National Automated Index Lookout System (NAILS), 64, 65
National Crime Information Center's Interstate Identification Index
(NCIC-III), 46
National Performance Review, 54
National Security Entry/Exit Registration System (NSEERS), 66, 72, 73,
74, 75, 76, 77, 78, 79, 91, 92, 94, 156,
162, 171

Non-Governmental Organizations (NGO), 133, 134, 136, 137, 144, 146

O

Office of Refugee Resettlement (ORR), 137, 148
Operation Liberty Shield, 155, 156

P

Padilla, Jose, 43, 166
Pakistan, 11, 73, 156
Palestinian Islamic Jihad (PIJ), 3
Permanent Residency (LPR), 4, 8, 9, 12, 13, 152, 153
Political Influences on the INS, 61
Population, Refugees, and Migration, Bureau of (PRM), 132, 134, 135, 136, 139, 152
Powell, Colin, 51, 112, 161, 171

R

Rahman, Sheik Omar Abdel, 5, 6, 7, 8, 9, 19, 28, 30, 151
Refugee Access Verification Unit (RA-VU), 149
Refugee Admission Ceiling, 136, 137
Refugees, 82, 131, 132, 134, 136, 139, 147
Reid, Richard, 41, 66
Reno, Janet, 9, 40
Resettlement, 133, 134, 136, 146, 151
Ridge, Tom, 95, 154, 156, 162
Rumsfeld, Donald, 77

S

Safe Third Country Agreement, 153, 154
Salameh, Mohammed, 5, 13, 17, 18
Saudi Arabia, 2, 71, 73, 156
Section 245(i) - See Immigration and Nationality Act
Secure Borders, Open Doors, 112
See Visas, P-3
State Department, 5, 6, 7, 8, 28, 86, 90, 126, 174
Student and Exchange Visitor Information System (SEVIS), 31, 47
Student and Exchange Visitor Program (SEVP), 103, 104, 105, 106, 120, 128
Supreme Court, 36, 39, 166

T

Tanzania, 2, 32, 46
Technology Alert List, 87, 88, 89
Terrorism Exclusion List, 27
Tourism, 94
Treasury Enforcement Communication System (TECS), 64, 65

U

U.S.S. Cole, 2, 46
United Association for Studies and Research (UASR), 4
United Nations, 5, 8, 136
United Nations High Commissioner of Refugees (UNHCR), 131, 134, 136, 137, 144, 146
United States Visitor and Immigrant Status Indicator Technology (US-VIS-IT), 47, 66, 71, 72, 91, 92, 93, 162
US Department of Justice, 62, 104
USA PATRIOT Act, 22, 42, 43, 44, 45, 46, 47, 67, 108, 109, 122, 123, 125, 139, 144, 148, 160, 164
USA PATRIOT Act II (Domestic Security Enhancement Act of 2003), 164
USCIS (Citizenship and Immigration Service), 50, 56, 64, 66, 135, 145, 155, 160, 161, 168

V

Visa Donkey, 87
Visa Eagle, 87
Visa issuance delays, 150
Visa Mantis, 86-91
Visa Waiver Program (VWP), 41, 64, 65
Visas
  F Visas (Student), 102, 106, 107
  H Visas (Work), 45, 161
  J Visas (Exchange Visitors), 102,106
  M Visas (Vocational Training), 102, 106, 107, 116
  P-3, 146, 147, 149, 150
  Tourist Visas, 6, 7, 14, 17, 30, 36, 41, 105
Visa 93 Provision, 147

W

Walker, John, 166
World and Islamic Studies Enterprise
    (WISE), 3
World Trade Center, 1, 5, 12, 32, 104, 108
Worldwide Refugee Admissions Pro-
    cessing System (WRAPS), 145

Y

Yousef, Ramzi, 9, 32, 71, 151

Z

Ziglar, James, 57, 59